Fast Fiction

Creating Fiction
in Five Minutes

Fast Fiction

Creating Fiction
in Five Minutes

ROBERTA ALLEN

STORY PRESS
CINCINNATI, OHIO

Fast Fiction: Creating Fiction in Five Minutes. Copyright © 1997 by Roberta Allen. Printed and bound in the United States of America. All rights reserved. No part of this book may be reproduced in any form or by any electronic or mechanical means including information storage and retrieval systems without permission in writing from the publisher, except by a reviewer, who may quote brief passages in a review. Published by Story Press, an imprint of F&W Publications, Inc., 1507 Dana Avenue, Cincinnati, Ohio 45207. (800) 289-0963. First edition.

Story Press Books are available from your local bookstore or direct from the publisher.

01 00 99 98 97   5 4 3 2 1

Library of Congress Cataloging-in-Publication Data

Allen, Roberta.
    Fast fiction : creating fiction in five minutes / Roberta Allen.
        p.   cm.
    Includes index.
    ISBN 1-884910-27-0 (hardcover : alk. paper)
    1. Short story. I. Title.
PN3373.A635   1997
808.3′1—dc21   97-10956
                                                               CIP

Designed by Clare Finney

The permissions on the next two pages constitute an extension of this copyright page.

PERMISSIONS

"Meeting" by Nomi Altabef is reprinted by permission of the author.

"Canton, Ohio: 1956" by Katherine Arnoldi is reprinted by permission of the author. Originally appeared in *The Quarterly* no. 18, summer 1991.

"The Decision to Part" and the exercise by Susan Bassik are reprinted by permission of the author. Copyright © 1995 by Susan Bassik.

"Bee-Keeping" by Greg Boyd is reprinted by permission of the author. Originally appeared in *Carnival Aptitude: Being an Exuberance in Short Prose and Photomontage* by Greg Boyd (Asylum Arts, 1993).

"Buddy" by Debbie Chapnick is reprinted by permission of the author. Copyright © 1996 by Debbie Chapnick.

The exercise by Elizabeth Conn is reprinted by permission of the author. Copyright © 1996 by Elizabeth Conn.

Exercises by Kim Connell are reprinted by permission of the author. Copyright © 1996 by Kim Connell.

Exercises by Donald Corken are reprinted by permission of the author. Copyright © 1996 by Donald Corken.

"My Sister and the Queen of England" by Lydia Davis is reprinted by permission of the author. Originally appeared in *The World* no. 48, 1993.

Exercises by Stephanie Dickinson are reprinted by permission of the author.

Story excerpt by Diane Doherty is reprinted by permission of the author. Copyright © 1995 by Diane Doherty.

"Dinner Time" by Russell Edson is reprinted by permission of the author. Copyright © 1964 by Russell Edson.

"Waiting" by Josephine Foo is reprinted by permission of the author. Originally appeared in *Open City* vol. 1, 1993.

"The Colonel" by Carolyn Forché is reprinted by permission of the author from *The Country Between Us* (HarperCollins, 1987).

Story endings by Peter Galperin are reprinted by permission of the author. Copyright © 1996 by Peter Galperin.

"Secret" by Morison Gampel is reprinted by permission of the author. Copyright © 1995 by Morison Gampel.

"Greed" and "The Tea Party" by Amanda Gardner are reprinted by permission of the author.

Story excerpts by David W. Harrison are reprinted by permission of the author. Copyright © 1995 by David W. Harrison.

Excerpts from "Rosary" by Robert Kelly are reprinted courtesy of McPherson & Company from the collection *A Transparent Tree* by Robert Kelly, copyright © 1985.

For all my students

ACKNOWLEDGMENTS

All my students—whether directly or indirectly—played a role in the shaping of this book. I am particularly indebted to the students in my private Monday and Wednesday evening workshops, whose enthusiasm for this project kept me going, and to the students in my Special Sunday Intensives, who tested methods outlined in the section on longer fiction. I wish to express my appreciation as well to my students at The New School, New York University, and The Writer's Voice, some of whom contributed as much to this project as my private students.

CONTENTS

PART I

THE SHORT SHORT STORY

ONE

AN INTRODUCTION

I remember the exact moment in 1981 when I made a decision that changed my life. I was in an art gallery in Rome. The occasion was the opening of my nineteenth solo exhibition. It was an odd moment to make a change, but standing there I knew that what I wanted to do most in life was write. My visual art combined words and images, so this decision was not as shocking as it sounds, and in truth, I never gave up art completely. Writing, however, has taken precedence since that time.

I had begun writing stories a year or two before my show in Rome. Initially, they seemed to come to me out of the blue. They were only a page or two in length, some even shorter. I carried a notebook with me everywhere I went so I could record them quickly. I would be walking down the street, for instance, when a memory would be triggered—by what I was not sure—and I would suddenly feel the urge to write. That urge was like a pressure. It was very intense. It weighed on me until I let the words out.

I had never heard of short short stories, but I seemed to be writing them, or, to be more exact, they seemed to be writing themselves. I was only the conduit. I was only the one holding the pen. Could writing really be this easy? I asked myself. It was after the stories found their way to paper that the real work began: the process of refining them. But this "work," as I called it, was much more fun than anything else I had ever called work. Because the stories were so short, I wasn't afraid to play around, try things out. The small scale kept them from being intimidating. At any moment, I could see the whole story or I could zoom in on a single part. While refining them I learned about the craft and discipline of writing fiction. This is not to say that revisions were easy, though sometimes they were. In some stories I had only to change a few words. Others required many drafts. But even when a story required major revision, I rarely if ever felt overwhelmed the way I might have if the story had been longer.

Later, after my first book of short short stories was published and I had occasion to teach a creative writing class at Parsons School of Design, I wondered how others might tap this unconscious source as I had, and learn the fundamentals of writing fiction at the same time. As an artist who had started drawing at age three, I was used to tapping my unconscious. Drawings happened. I didn't think about them. I didn't plan them. The first drafts of my stories seemed to happen in the same way. I wondered if I could trigger this process in others.

Discovering the Five-Minute Process

At Parsons, my first students were art students. They had never written stories before. Like most people who have never written fiction, they came to class with certain expectations, preconceptions, and fears. My first task was to clear their minds and get them to a state I call "ground zero." I did this by using photographic images projected on a screen. I picked the images carefully. The photographs hinted at stories rather than telling them. In other words, there was always room for the student to project his dreams, fantasies, thoughts, and feelings. Students were amazed to find that in five-minute exercises, they were able to write complete drafts of short short stories, triggered by the projected images. They even began to enjoy the process of revision after they realized that here was an arena for play as well as for learning.

While revising stories at home, each student became aware of her own writing process. This is important because it is different for each of us. When I talk about this process, I mean everything that has to do with writing, including the place where the student prefers to work, the time of day, whether she uses a computer or writes in longhand, how much time the student usually spends at one sitting. I will say more about the process later. It is only important here to note that my course at Parsons allowed me to see how different it was for each student.

After my course at Parsons, I decided to expand my repertoire of exercises to include verbal directives, such as "Write a story about a lie," as well as visual cues. I wondered how this method would work for people who were not artists, who were not used to tuning in on their unconscious minds. This question was answered when I was hired to teach a course in short short stories for adults at The Writer's Voice, an alternative literary center at the West Side YMCA in New York. There wasn't a projector so I used no visual images at all. Employing only verbal directives, I found the five-minute exercises worked as well for lawyers, actors, consultants, plumbers, grandmothers, journalists, secretaries, and retired policemen as they did for art students. In fact, the people in my class were more than happy to turn off the part of their minds that balances their checkbooks, pays bills, makes trips to the dry cleaners, and tends to all the other mundane details of life.

When I began teaching at The New School for Social Research and New York University a year later, I used projected images and verbal cues in the five-minute exercises. By that time, I had learned something else: Writing is energy, psychic energy. When the desire to write is really strong, there's lots of energy in that desire. The more energy the better. The five-minute exercises seemed to focus that energy. I learned that in the beginning, energy is far more important than skill. The craft of writing can be learned, but that energy, kindled by desire, is the "spirit" and "fire" of fiction. Without it, writing is dead.

From the time I began writing short short stories until my first book, *The Traveling Woman*, was published, I read many very short fictions by a wide variety of writers, from the great German-language authors Franz Kafka and Robert Walser, to Ernest Hemingway and Joyce Carol Oates, to South American writer Luisa Valenzuela.

Here is one of Kafka's shorter stories. They don't get much more concise than this.

A LITTLE FABLE
by Franz Kafka

"Alas," said the mouse, "the world is growing smaller every day. At the beginning it was so big that I was afraid, I kept running and running, and I was glad when at last I saw walls far away to the right and left, but these long walls have narrowed so quickly that I am in the last chamber already, and there in the corner stands the trap that I must run into." "You only need to change your direction," said the cat, and ate it up.

I found that few writers used this form exclusively, but many wrote short shorts from time to time. I reread experimentalist Italo Calvino's *Invisible Cities*, a novel made up of stories that are a page or two in length. I discovered *Einstein's Dreams*, by physicist and author Alan Lightman, a more recent novel composed of short shorts, each a few pages long. There were other novels as well that made use of the very short form, such as *The House on Mango Street*, by Sandra Cisneros. In the meantime, I had written *The Daughter*, a novella in short short stories, as well as several longer fictions, all composed of short shorts. Once I started looking, I found more novels with chapters of five pages or less. Though the quality of the writing varied and the chapters did not conform to my idea of short shorts, which are stories complete in themselves even when they are part of something longer, I saw another possibility: I knew that linking short shorts could create an original form of fiction. I also knew this special form was not for everyone. I began to wonder if the five-minute exercises could be used to write more than short shorts.

I asked myself many questions. How, for example, could one exercise generate another? How could they be part of a greater plan? How could they be linked? All sorts of answers came to mind. There could be many different exercises on a single theme, for instance, or the same story could be told from many points of view. The possibilities seemed to multiply. This book, which uses the five-minute method to introduce you to a quick and easy way of writing fiction, was born out of those possibilities.

WHAT TO EXPECT

You may be quite happy to use this book to do nothing more than learn to write short short stories. That's fine. You may appreciate the short short form on its own for as long as you like. No one is rushing you. Finding the pace that suits you is part of discovering your writing process.

I can tell you in advance that you will not be spending your time and energy wondering what to write and how to write it. The five-minute exercises will take care of that. The words will flow faster than you can imagine. You have already accumulated more stories in your mind than you will ever find time to use. These stories will surprise you. They are not the ones you expected to write. They live in a deeper place in your mind—in your unconscious. Like an oilman, you will dig deep inside your well and bring forth riches. The difference is that the oilman is working a lot harder than you will be. It is not effort that brings forth stories from the unconscious; it is the act of allowing them to come forth. Or I can say it another way: It's the act of stepping aside from your rational, logical mind and allowing the other mind to take over. This deeper mind is not bound by rules. It is free and creative. If you are asking how you can step aside from your rational mind, you are still holding on to it. Fortunately, you will not have occasion to ask that question (or any other question, for that matter) while you are doing exercises. In five minutes, you don't have time to ask questions and make judgments. You don't have time to do anything but write.

By the time you are ready to tackle a longer fiction or a novel, writing exercises will be second nature to you. You will be comfortable with tapping your unconscious. You will also have developed a degree of technical skill and discipline that comes from taking the initial exercise or first draft through a number of revisions until you are satisfied with the result. Many of the common problems you will encounter in writing longer fictions, such as needless repetition, lack of tension, or an illogical sequence of events, will be familiar. You will have encountered these problems while revising the short short, which will have enabled you to see those problems in perspective, in miniature. And remember, you will be working part by part. It's hard to feel overwhelmed when you can zoom in and focus on a particular segment. Even if you get stuck on one segment for a while, you can go on to another. It's hard to be intimidated by something that is small, even if you have tried in the past to write fiction and were unhappy with the results.

WHO IS A BEGINNING WRITER?

This question is not as silly as it may sound. In reading this book, it is important that you see yourself as a beginner, see yourself at "ground zero" even if you are an experienced writer. If you do other kinds of writing, such as journalism or technical writing, using this book will require an about-face on your part, at least in the beginning. Whether you are a journalist, an electrician, or an investment banker, you probably have expectations about what should happen and fears, perhaps, about trying something new.

It's exciting to start something new. It's also scary. It's okay to be scared. In fact, the more scared you are the better. There's a lot of energy in being scared, and you want to have as much energy available as possible. You want that energy to flow from your fingers through your pen or pencil or through your keyboard. You want it to leap off the page. You want the reader to connect with it. So think of your fear as a place to begin.

Perhaps this is not your first beginning. Maybe you already have tried writing fiction or have completed one or more stories in the past, but for whatever reasons, you haven't written anything since. You feel out of shape. You need to find your way back to your writing.

Or perhaps you have made many attempts at writing fiction. You were doing fine for a while but then stopped. You reached a point where you didn't know how to go further. You felt lost, perhaps, or blocked. Or maybe you felt overwhelmed when you saw how much effort it would take. Why am I doing this? you asked yourself. You couldn't find a good enough "reason" to continue so you lost interest and put the work in a file full of unfinished stories.

What you may not be aware of is the other file, the one in your mind that is constantly accumulating thoughts, feelings, dreams, fantasies, memories, wishes. Stored there are fleeting glances, sunrises, sunsets, the textures and colors of lived experience. That file is meant only for you. Think of this book as your key to the file when the urge to write fiction comes back.

Perhaps that's the problem: No matter how many times you swear you will never write fiction again, the urge always comes back. The urge may be as unwanted as malaria, but it is something you cannot ignore. It forces you to take action. It may have forced you, for example, to buy this book. Your rational mind may think that writing fiction is not worth the effort, but your intuitive mind knows better and is ready once more to begin.

It isn't necessary to have a problem to use this method. You may simply be curious. You may want to try something new, something different. You are interested in finding an easier or faster way to tune in on yourself and get your stories or novels on paper. Perhaps you have achieved some success. Maybe you've published several stories or novels.

Or perhaps you have always wanted to write fiction, but you've never found time. Or you start stories but never find time to finish. Something always comes up in your life to keep you from writing.

Let's face it. Life will always get in the way of writing fiction because that's how life is. The good things that happen may get in the way as much as the bad. If you win the lottery, for example, you'll probably forget about writing fiction for a while—you'll be too busy spending all that money. Or you might fall in love. There are times when fiction seems dull and drab compared to life. It's important to honor your feelings.

In fact, not having time to write fiction may be good for your writing. When the urge to write is strong but you feel you can't do anything about it, the energy builds inside you. I've found it helpful to wait sometimes until the urge is really strong before I begin. Next time you feel frustrated about not having time to write, think about that energy building. You may find, however, you spend far less time feeling frustrated once you allow yourself to release that energy in five-minute bursts. The five minutes you spend skimming through a magazine or staring out the window is the same five minutes you can use to complete an exercise. Perhaps you will find five or six times in a day to take five minutes out from your busy schedule. If you've been waiting a long time to write, the words will probably gush forth if you let them.

You are a beginning writer if you allow yourself to be. It doesn't matter how many times you have tried in the past. What makes you a beginner is not your lack of experience, your lack of expertise, or what you may consider your lack of success. It is your willingness to be open, to make a fresh start.

Each new project demands a new beginning. Ideally, the writer starts "stupid." The more stupid you can be, the better. For example, when Chris, one of my students, started a novel, he wasn't stupid enough. He realized later that in the back of his mind, he was trying to impress his mother, though his mother had no idea he was writing a novel and he had no intention of telling her. In his mind, he was trying to show her how smart he was. He was using a vocabulary he didn't normally use. The words didn't ring true. They were out of tone

(I will talk more about this later). But when he let himself be "stupid," Chris was able to tap his unconscious and write—without interfering with his writing process.

Some of you may find it difficult to begin with a clear mind. That's okay. Robert, another of my students, told me that sometimes even while he is doing exercises, he hears a voice in his head saying, "This is corny" or "Why are you writing this drivel?" He doesn't, however, let this voice stop him from capturing his story. You, too, may not be able to stop the chatter in your head, but, like Robert, you can learn not to listen.

WHAT YOU NEED TO KNOW BEFORE YOU BEGIN

I want you to think of a story or novel that moved you. How did you know you were moved? The story or novel gave you a feeling. What did the writer do to give you that feeling? He created a world you could enter. He opened a door and let you in.

It was also a feeling that made you realize that you want to write fiction. As a writer, it is important to pay close attention to what you feel. Very often, especially in the beginning, you may have difficulty revising your exercises because you have not yet learned to trust your feelings. In fact, some of you may not even know what you feel. You may only be aware of uncertainty or confusion or anxiety. These emotions may have little to do with your story, but it is important to recognize them and step back if they get in the way.

In advance, I will tell you a little game to play. I want you to ask yourself: What's so important about this story? If you don't get it right today or next week or ever, what's the big deal? Isn't this only one of many you will write? Close your eyes and imagine a thousand sheets of paper, each one covered with a story. Or imagine yourself in a plane, looking down on your life. What do you see? Do you see the town where you live? Do you see your house? Are there family and friends below? What else do you see? Where is your story in relation to all that you see? Now ask yourself this: What changes would you make if you weren't uncertain or anxious or confused?

The process of revision can be fun when you recognize it as an opportunity to play. This book is full of games you can play while learning the craft of fiction. But you need to be willing to play them.

Pay Attention to Your Feelings and Energy

The more you write the more you will learn to trust what you feel. In the beginning, whether or not your decisions improve the story is secondary. What is most important is that you make decisions even though you are unsure. There will probably be times when the changes you make are far off the track. On the other hand, don't be surprised if your best revisions originate in missteps. You must allow yourself to go astray. You must allow yourself to "ruin" your story, though of course it is impossible to ruin a story since you can always go back and change it.

So how will you know if a change you made doesn't work? You will know by the way it makes you feel. You already know how it feels to be moved by a story. You have a model for comparison. If you're unsure, you need to put your work aside so you can return to it fresh at a later time. Meanwhile, you can go on to revising the next one. The more you revise the more aware you will be of what I call "pinpricks" of feeling. These are subtle sensations that call your attention to precise places in your stories that need work. You may think of these sensations as your very own "radar." They tell you where a piece has gone dead or where a word choice could be better or even when a comma is out of place.

It is important to remember, especially in the beginning, that the words in an exercise are less important than the energy behind those words. Wherever you have energy, you have the seed of a story or novel, even if it is only a phrase or a sentence that excites you.

While reworking your exercises, you will try to keep the initial energy that sparked them. Despite your best efforts, there will probably be times when your exercise will lose that spark and go dead. This is not a catastrophe. It means you have gone in the wrong direction and need to go back to the starting point and try again. It is important that you judge none of your missteps as wasted efforts. Every chance you take will yield some useful information even if you don't see it at that moment. Your mind will be absorbing more than you know.

It is important for you to time the exercises. This will keep your mind on your writing. You won't have a chance to censure yourself or let judgments and preconceived notions get in your way. You let your mind go where it will when you allow your unconscious to take over.

The exercises may be used again and again. You can probably draft at least ten stories, for instance, from the exercise "Write a story about a chair." Throughout the book, I suggest various ways to choose exercises and various games you may play with them. The idea is to have fun, to make this process as exciting for yourself as possible.

Doing exercises shouldn't feel like drudgery. If from time to time it does, this may be part of your particular process, or it may have nothing at all to do with your writing. You may be weighed down, for example, by problems in your life that are interfering. Instead of allowing those problems to get you down, use them in your exercises. Let them take center stage rather than stand in the wings, casting shadows. There's real energy there. How you feel mentally and physically will affect how you write. While this book is not about fiction writing as therapy, it is about using whatever comes up. The process can be cathartic.

If you still wonder how you'll go from exercises to finished stories, you may liken each exercise to Cinderella in rags. The beauty she will become at the ball is already contained within her. So it is with fiction. The finished stories are there within your exercises. But it may take you some time and fiddling to tease them out. You will be called upon to use the conscious part of your mind just when you were getting comfortable tapping your unconscious. This doesn't mean, however, that you will stop using the unconscious. On the contrary, you will be like a juggler, going back and forth between the two, juggling both parts of your mind.

Perhaps it is because of my visual art background that I see these exercises as blocks of wood or stone, ready to be carved. You will have an advantage over the sculptor, however. The sculptor cannot bring back wood or stone he has chipped away. As a writer, you can always bring back words.

I will add here that solutions I present to common problems are by no means the only ones possible. In fact, I encourage you to try several different approaches in working out trouble spots so you may see which ones work best for you.

In these pages, I have presented a number of definitions of the short short story. I could have given you more. Almost every author of short shorts seems to have a particular way of defining them. Even the qualities of brevity, unexpectedness, and intensity, which I present here as the unique qualities of the very short story, may not be agreed upon by all those who write them. I find this a wonderful state of affairs. Definitions often limit possibility. In this case, the short short is still open to definition, still open to further exploration as it were. Think of yourself as an explorer as you follow the path I've laid out for you. Have fun along the way.

Model Stories

I have included a number of published short shorts to use as models. Written by a variety of authors, these stories will give some idea of how different one story can be from another. The moods they express, the shapes they take, are as varied as the form itself. By showing you the kinds of stories that already exist, I wish to share with you this spirit of possibility, this sense that almost anything can happen within the small space of a short short.

On your own, you may come across stories that don't fit neatly into the categories. That's fine. There are no "real" categories when all is said and done. They simply offer a way to point up similarities and differences.

Playing With Possibilities

As I think you realize by now, this book is about playing with possibilities so that ultimately you will make the right fictional choices for yourself, the ones that "feel" right. *Energy, feeling,* and *the writing process* are the key words in these pages. If you learn to follow your feelings and go where the energy is, you will learn a great deal about your writing process. When you know a great deal about that, you know a great deal about yourself. The more self-knowledge you have, the more you bring of yourself to your fiction.

The main strategy I present in this book may be compared with my strategy for climbing down pyramids in Mexico and mountains in Peru. I am afraid of heights, but I love the views and the spiritual feeling I have when looking out at raw nature. What scares me about high places is coming down. When I see how far I have to go to reach the bottom, I tell myself, "I can't do this." But I discovered something: If I keep my eyes focused on my next step when I start my descent, I'm less afraid. By concentrating my attention on one step at a time, before I know it I am back on level ground.

Writing a novel or longer fiction may seem to you as frightening or overwhelming or impossible as climbing down a mountain. But if you see your novel as a number of small parts, it's less likely to produce these feelings, especially if you focus on one part at a time. When you see the novel or long fiction you are about to write as a series of short parts, it is suddenly manageable. The French philosopher Gaston Bachelard said, "The cleverer I am at miniaturizing the world, the better I possess it."

I have seen people start out writing novels with great bursts of vitality, but that one great burst usually peters out long before the book is finished. You can't depend on a single spurt to carry you through a long piece of work. Novels and most longer fictions are written over time, and as such they cannot be rushed.

The experience of writing a novel will be quite different from that of writing a short short story, though the novel will contain within it the experience of writing the short short. There will be new considerations that didn't come up when dealing exclusively with very short stories. How, for example, do you create the suspense necessary to keep the reader's interest? How do you keep a narrative moving that is written in short parts? How do you decide what ties the stories together? How do you develop characters and theme? How do you plot a longer fiction or novel? How can you see the whole while working part by part? You will be given examples of solutions and a number of possibilities to try on your own. By trying various approaches, you will learn more about your own writing process.

A FEW WORDS ABOUT RULES

There are no "real" rules for writing short shorts, just as there are no "real" rules for writing longer fiction, but there are methods to help you find your way. Your "way" is not anyone else's way. Find what works for you. Discover and honor your writing process. This process is not fixed; it is living and moving inside you.

Having said this doesn't stop me from also saying that the most successful short shorts share the particular qualities presented in this book. Without these qualities, a short short probably won't work. I say probably because it's possible I'll be surprised. Surprise is one of the short short's primary features.

When I say there are no "real" rules, I mean that they are not carved in stone. I believe rules are meant to be broken, but only after they are learned. There is a reason for them. They focus the mind. The methods laid down in this book are easy to follow, easy to learn, and they work if you use them. If you need to rebel, it's easier to rebel against something you know. So my advice would be to learn as much as you can first. Then go for it. Ultimately, what counts is whether your story or novel "works." How you got there is beside the point. Exactly what happened may never be known. You may not be able to follow your own trail twice. That's the way stories and novels are sometimes. They are words plus a little bit of magic.

THE VARIETY OF SHORT SHORT STORIES

Short short stories have become increasingly popular in the last decade. You may find them in literary journals as well as in the new 'zines, which publish the work of young writers. Several anthologies are devoted to them. They have even graced the pages of *The New Yorker* and *Vanity Fair*. Twenty years ago, however, this forest of short shorts was a desert. Finding fiction under five pages was difficult. Fifty years ago, the presence of these little stories in magazines was nothing out of the ordinary. What happened in the years in between? Did writers stop writing them? Or did publishers stop publishing them?

The answer is anybody's guess. It's easy to see, however, why the form would be popular now. In our fast-paced age, as people have shorter and shorter attention spans and little time to read, the short short is perfect. Some stories are brief enough to be read in the time it takes to watch a television commercial. Take this surreal little piece by contemporary writer Greg Boyd, for instance. Aside from being short, it is sharply focused and surprising. The author creates a world in less than a hundred words.

BEE-KEEPING
by Greg Boyd

A giant bee flies through the window of my bedroom, lands on my chest and regurgitates a sickly sweet liquid into my mouth. After it leaves, I realize it has turned my bed to wax. With difficulty I wriggle loose from stiff sheets, pull myself onto my feet, and escape into a world of sunlight and flowers.

Even fifty years ago, the short short form was far from new. Fables, folk tales, parables, and prose poems are precursors of the form.

I have not limited the selections in this chapter to those written in the present, though the ones I have chosen from the past, Anton Chekhov's "The Nincompoop" (1883), which takes place in Russia, and Swiss writer Robert Walser's story "Nothing At All" (1917), have a contemporary ring. The others were written by contemporary fiction writers and poets. All the stories are under a thousand words.

These few samples only *suggest* the variety of short shorts. I suspect several hundred pages would be necessary to give an accurate picture of the true variety. Instead of trying to do the impossible, I have selected stories I respond to: those that work for me. In the following pages, I will discuss what makes them work.

You may not respond to all of these selections, or you may find at different times, you respond to different ones. That's fine. What is important is being aware of how you *feel* about a given short short. When you are moved, ask yourself what moves you. Look for it. Listen to it. See this chapter as part of the process of training yourself to pay attention to how you feel.

NOTHING AT ALL
by Robert Walser

A woman who was only just a little flighty went to town to buy something good for supper for herself and her husband. Of course, many a woman has gone shopping and in so doing been just a little absentminded. So in no way is this story new; all the same, I shall continue and relate that the woman who had wanted to buy something good for supper for herself and her husband and for this reason had gone to town did not exactly have her mind on the matter. Over and over she considered what delights and delicacies she could buy for herself and her husband, but since she didn't, as already mentioned, exactly have her mind on the matter and was a little absentminded, she came to no decision, and it seemed that she did not exactly know what she really wanted. "It must be something that can be made quickly since it's already late, my time is limited," she thought. God! She was, you know, only just a little flighty and did not exactly have her mind on the matter. Impartiality and objectivity are fine and good. But the woman here was not particularly objective, rather a little absentminded and flighty. Over and over she considered but came, as already mentioned, to no decision. The ability to make a decision is fine and good. But this woman possessed no such ability. She wanted to buy something really good and delicious for herself and her husband to eat. And for this fine reason she went to town; but she simply did not succeed, she simply did not succeed. Over and over she considered. She wasn't lacking in good will, she certainly wasn't lacking in good intentions, she was just a little flighty, didn't have her mind on the matter, and therefore didn't succeed. It isn't good when minds aren't on the matter, and, in a word, the woman finally got disgusted, and she went home with nothing at all.

"What delicious and good, exquisite and fine, sensible and intelligent food did you buy for supper?" asked the husband when he saw his good-looking, nice little wife come home.

She replied: "I bought nothing at all."

"How's that?" asked the husband.

She said: "Over and over I considered, but came to no decision, because the choice was too difficult for me to make. Also it was already late, and my time was limited. I wasn't lacking in good will or the best of all intentions, but I just didn't have my mind on the matter. Believe me, dear husband, it's really terrible when you don't keep your mind on a matter. It seems that I was only just a little flighty and because of that I didn't succeed. I went to town and I wanted to buy something truly delicious and good for me and you, I wasn't lacking in good will, over and over I considered, but the choice was too difficult and my mind wasn't on the matter, and therefore I didn't succeed, and therefore I bought nothing at all. We will have to be satisfied today with nothing at all for once, won't we. Nothing at all can be prepared most quickly and, at any rate, doesn't cause indigestion. Should you be angry with me for this? I can't believe that."

So for once, or for a change, they ate nothing at all at night, and the good upright husband was in no way angry, he was too chivalrous, too mannerly, and too well-behaved for that. He would never have dared to make an unpleasant face, he was much too cultivated. A good husband doesn't do something like that. And so they ate nothing at all and were both satisfied, for it tasted exceptionally good to them. His wife's idea to prefer nothing at all for a change the good husband found quite charming, and while he maintained that he was convinced she had had a delightful inspiration, he feigned his great joy, whereby he indeed concealed how welcome a nutritious, honest supper like, e.g., a hearty, valiant apple mash would have been.

Many other things would have probably tasted better to him than nothing at all.

In this short short, a wife can't decide what to buy her husband for dinner so she winds up buying him nothing. What happens—or doesn't happen in this case—is far less interesting than the voice telling it. The voice is sly and mocking, but even while the narrator mocks the wife's indecisiveness and the husband's "chivalrous" behavior, he is sympathetic toward them. Walser uses repetition to mirror the wife's state of mind: a painful state of indecisiveness. Using such phrases as "Over and over she considered," the prose goes round and round, coming to no conclusion. We end up with a picture of a state of consciousness rather than a picture of a particular human being. Neither character is realistically portrayed. The wife and her husband are the embodiment of conventional values, but Walser presents them in an unconventional way. His use of trite words and phrases mocks these values when he speaks, for example, of "good will" and "good intentions," "the good upright husband," or "his good-looking, nice little wife," while revealing at the same time the wife's angst and the husband's deception. The characters speak in the same voice as the narrator (note the wife's speech to the husband and the husband's brief words to his wife), instead of having varied voices the way characters in realistic stories do. We don't know these characters as individuals, yet we are able to see inside them and understand them because they represent universal states of being.

THE NINCOMPOOP
by Anton Chekhov

The other day I called to my office the governess of my children, Julia Vasilevna. It was time to settle accounts.

"Please be seated, Julia Vasilevna," I said to her. "We must do some calculating. Certainly you need money, but you have such good manners that you do not make a request . . . Now. . . . We agreed upon thirty rubles a month . . ."

"Upon forty . . ."

"No, upon thirty . . . I have it recorded. . . . I have always paid the governesses thirty rubles. . . . Let's see, you have spent two months here. . . ."

"Two months and five days . . ."

"Exactly two months . . . I have it recorded. It means you are entitled to sixty rubles. . . . Subtract nine Sundays—you know you were not occupied with Kolya on Sundays, and only went strolling—and three holidays. . . ."

Julia Vasilevna flushed and wanted to have a chance to protest but . . . not a word from her!

"Three holidays. Subtract, it follows, twelve rubles. . . . Four days when Kolya was sick and you were free of him and only had Vara. . . . You had a toothache for three days and my wife permitted you to be free after dinner. . . . That's twelve plus seven—nineteen. Deduct . . . that leaves . . . hmm . . . forty-one rubles. Correct?"

Julia Vasilevna's left eye reddened and became moist. Her chin quivered. She coughed nervously, blew her nose, but— not a word from her! . . .

"On New Year's Eve you broke a china cup and saucer. Subtract two rubles. . . . The cup is much more valuable—it is a family heirloom, but . . . we'll forget about that! What haven't we lost! Later, because you did not keep your eyes on Kolya, he climbed a tree and tore his jacket. . . . Subtract ten. . . . The maid, also because you were negligent and did not watch her, stole Vara's boots. You must be responsible for everything. You are paid a salary. And so, this means, another five rubles must be subtracted. . . . On the tenth of January I gave you ten rubles. . . ."

"I didn't get them!" whispered Julia Vasilevna.

"But I have it recorded!"

"Oh, well . . . forget it."

"From forty-one rubles subtract twenty-seven—this leaves fourteen."

Both her eyes were now full of tears. . . . Perspiration appeared on the long, pretty little nose. Poor girl!

"Only once was I given anything," she said with a quivering voice. "I had three rubles from your wife. . . . No more. . . ."

"Really? Wouldn't you know it, I don't have it recorded! Subtract three from fourteen and that leaves eleven rubles. . . . Here's your money, my pretty one! Three . . . three, three . . . and one . . . Take it please!"

And I gave her eleven rubles. . . . She took them with shaking fingers and put them in her pocket.

"*Merci*," she whispered.

I jumped up and paced the room. I was overcome with anger.

"What are you saying *merci* for?" I asked.

"For the money . . ."

"But you know I fleeced you, damn it, robbed you! You know I stole from you! For this you thank me?"

"In other places I was not given all . . ."

"Not given? And not so subtly! I was playing a joke on you, teaching you a cruel lesson. I will give you all eighty rubles I owe you! They are ready for you in this envelope! But, is it possible that such meanness is common? Why didn't you protest? Why are you silent? Is it possible that on this earth there is one so slow to respond? Is it possible that there really is such a nincompoop?"

She smiled bitterly, and I could see from her face: "It is possible!"

I asked for her forgiveness for the cruel lesson and to her great amazement gave her the eighty rubles. She shyly *mercied* me and left. . . . My eyes watched her leave and I thought: "How easy it is to be strong in this world!"

A man pretends to cheat his governess in order to teach her a lesson. He tries to provoke her by reducing her wages, bit by bit, until there is almost nothing left. Still, she doesn't protest. She allows him to steal her money. Compare the more distant third-person narrator in Walser's story with the immediacy of the first-person narrator in this one. Here, the characters are revealed mostly through dialogue. We are given little description, but when Chekhov does describe the governess by saying, for example, her ". . . left eye reddened and became moist. Her chin quivered. She coughed nervously . . . ," he gives us in very few words a precise picture of the woman at that moment. Since the tale is told from her employer's perspective, we see her only through his eyes, so our knowledge of the governess is limited. We cannot see inside her mind. Unlike Walser's characters, however, the narrator and the governess are realistically drawn; the dialogue feels as though real people are speaking: The voice of the governess, for instance, would never be mistaken for that of the narrator. Because the story is so brief, however, and nothing is known about the governess's life apart from her employment (though we may infer a great deal about her from this incident), she is an individual who represents powerlessness. What we learn about her relates only to this condition because this is the focus of the story.

THE COLONEL
by Carolyn Forché

What you have heard is true. I was in his house. His wife carried a tray of coffee and sugar. His daughter filed her nails, his son went out for the night. There were daily papers, pet dogs, a pistol on the cushion beside him. The moon swung bare on its black cord over the house. On the television was a cop show. It was in English. Broken bottles were embedded in the walls around the house to scoop the kneecaps from a man's legs or cut his hands to lace. On the windows there were gratings like those in liquor stores. We had dinner, rack of lamb, good wine, a gold bell was on the table for calling the maid. The maid brought green mangoes, salt, a type of bread. I was asked how I enjoyed the country. There was a brief commercial in Spanish. His wife took everything away. There was some talk then of how difficult it had become to govern. The parrot said hello on the terrace. The colonel told it to shut up, and pushed himself from the table. My friend said to me with his eyes: say nothing. The colonel returned with a sack used to bring groceries home. He spilled many human ears on the table. They were like dried peach halves. There is no other way to say this. He took one of them in his hands, shook it in our faces, dropped it into a water glass. It came alive there. I am tired of fooling around he said. As for the rights of anyone, tell your people they can go fuck themselves. He swept the ears to the floor with his arm and held the last of his wine in the air. Something for your poetry, no? he said. Some of the ears on the floor caught this scrap of his voice. Some of the ears on the floor were pressed to the ground.

While visiting the colonel's house, the poet-narrator is shown evidence of the colonel's brutality when he empties a bag of ears on the dinner table. This chilling visit is described in language that is simple, precise, and poetic. Short staccato sentences create a strong rhythm. Tension builds as the poet-narrator describes banal and horrifying details in the same tone. This short short, like Chekhov's, is told in first person, but unlike Chekhov's narrator, who tells us exactly how he feels when he says, for example, "I jumped up and paced the room. I was overcome with anger," Forché's narrator controls her emotion and evokes a sense of menace simply by describing what she sees, without comment. Take this sentence, for example: "Broken bottles were embedded in the walls around the house to scoop the kneecaps from a man's legs or cut his hands to lace." She acts as reporter, barely insinuating herself into the story, but she is not a neutral observer. Even while she keeps her distance by not directly revealing her thoughts and feelings, the urgency behind her words is evident. We feel the emotion. The sense of menace is heightened by the contrast between the story's harrowing content and minimal means. In response to the colonel's challenge, "Something for your poetry, no?" we see her sympathy for the victims, as she, in the last poetic images, brings them back to life.

VISION OUT OF THE CORNER OF ONE EYE
by Luisa Valenzuela

It's true, he put his hand on my ass and I was about to scream bloody murder when the bus passed by a church and he crossed himself. He's a good sort after all, I said to myself.

Maybe he didn't do it on purpose or maybe his right hand didn't know what his left hand was up to. I tried to move farther back in the bus—searching for explanations is one thing and letting yourself be pawed is another—but more passengers got on and there was no way I could do it. My wiggling to get out of his reach only let him get a better hold on me and even fondle me. I was nervous and finally moved over. He moved over, too. We passed by another church but he didn't notice it and when he raised his hand to his face it was to wipe the sweat off his forehead. I watched him out of the corner of one eye, pretending that nothing was happening, or at any rate not making him think I liked it. It was impossible to move a step farther and he began jiggling me. I decided to get even and put my hand on his behind. A few blocks later I got separated from him. Then I was swept along by the passengers getting off the bus and now I'm sorry I lost him so suddenly because there were only 7,400 pesos in his wallet and I'd have gotten more out of him if we'd been alone. He seemed affectionate. And very generous.

A woman who is molested on a bus gets her revenge by stealing money from the man molesting her. Like Forché's story, this one is told in first person and focuses on a single incident, described in language that is simple and precise. However, Valenzuela's narrator speaks directly to the reader with the immediacy of the employer in "The Nincompoop." The narrator sounds as though she's holding nothing back, but she is full of surprises, thwarting our expectations at every turn, defying convention and female stereotypes by creating a female character who, in the midst of a compromising sexual situation, retains her sense of humor and is neither passive nor powerless like Chekhov's governess. Valenzuela gives the story several twists. The first one occurs after the woman has been "pawed." She sees the man cross himself when they pass a church and responds by saying, "He's a good sort after all. . . ." A little later when he starts "jiggling" her, the author twists the story again when she says the narrator got even by putting her "hand on his behind." Each twist keeps the reader off balance by changing the story's direction until the final one at the end when we learn she has taken his money. The man molesting her is seen only through his actions. We know nothing else about him. He functions as a symbol or cipher rather than a real person. Though the distinctive voice of the narrator stamps her as an individual, we see only this little piece of her life, which is enough for the story, but if we ask ourselves who this woman is, we still don't know.

BLINDSIDED
by Don Shea

It started as a low, sweet jumble of sound, whiny and country, from the far end of the subway car. Then you could make out a small, pale man of middle years and thinning hair shuffling forward through the passengers with a dog by his side and a sack on his back containing a radio or tape player from which this strangely sweet country sound—a voice, a guitar and fiddle—was spilling out and he was singing along with it, singing along with his own voice or whoever's, singing softly in a nasal tenor as clear as spring water, and then you recognized the song, one of John Denver's impossibly sentimental ballads about home and hearth and supper on the stove that you were always ashamed of liking, but you would not be taken that easily—street smart New Yorker—and you searched his bowed head for fraud, searched out his eyes even as you reached for your loose change, and just then the small pale man drew abreast of you and threw back his head, and as his eyes came up milky and twisted and wrong, his face fused ecstatically and the purest sound came forth from him and struck something inside you that came undone, and you would have given great value at that moment to see what he saw, to see what lay beyond embarrassment.

The narrator is moved by the song of a panhandler in the subway. Shea uses the second-person *you*, which is an uncommon point of view. Here, *you* refers to the narrator, who is talking about himself, observing himself in relation to the panhandler, saying, for example, ". . . you searched his bowed head for fraud. . . ." At the same time, *you* feels inclusive, draws us into the narrator's experience so we can share in his revelation when he says the panhandler's song "struck something inside you that came undone." *You* makes us feel as though we are there. We identify with the narrator, who wants to see what the panhandler saw but can't get inside the man's head. The narrator can only describe what he sees, which he does in precise and economical language when he says the panhandler "threw back his head, and as his eyes came up milky and twisted and wrong, his face fused ecstatically and the purest sound came forth." Unlike the other stories so far, this one is composed of only two sentences. Shea uses the longer one, which holds most of the story, to build in one long sweep to the climax at the end. We know little about the narrator except that he is a "street smart New Yorker" who doesn't let himself be fooled. We see the panhandler as a blind man who is carried away by emotion as he sings. In the last lines, we feel a sense of longing in the narrator to be carried away by emotion like the panhandler. Without knowing anything else about them, we may feel as though we see deep inside these characters. We may feel as though we glimpse their souls.

SPACE
by Mark Strand

A beautiful woman stood at the roof-edge of one of New York's tall midtown apartment houses. She was on the verge of jumping when a man, coming out on the roof to sunbathe, saw her. Surprised, the woman stepped back from the ledge. The man was about thirty or thirty-five and blond. He was lean, with a long upper body and short, thin legs. His black bathing suit shone like satin in the sun. He was no more than ten steps from the woman. She stared at him. The wind blew strands of her long dark hair across her face. She pulled them back and held them in place with one hand. Her white blouse and pale blue skirt kept billowing, but she paid no attention. He saw that she was barefoot and that two high-heeled shoes were placed side by side on the gravel near where she stood. She had turned away from him. The wind flattened her skirt against the front of her long thighs. He wished he could reach out and pull her toward him. The air shifted and drew her skirt tightly across her small, round buttocks, the lines of her bikini underpants showed. "I'll take you to dinner," he yelled. The woman turned to look at him again. Her gaze was point-blank. Her teeth were clenched. The man looked at her hands which were now crossed in front of her, holding her skirt in place. She wore no wedding band. "Let's go someplace and talk," he said. She took a deep breath and turned away. She lifted her arms as if she were preparing to dive. "Look," he said, "if it's me you're worried about, you have nothing to fear." He took the towel he was carrying over his shoulders and made it into a sarong. "I know it's depressing," he said. He was not sure what he had meant. He wondered if the woman felt anything. He liked the way her back curved into her buttocks. It struck him as simple and expressive; it suggested an appetite or potential for sex. He wished he could touch her. As if to give him some hope, the woman lowered her arms to her sides and shifted her weight. "I'll tell you what," the man said, "I'll marry you." The wind once again pulled the woman's skirt tightly across her buttocks. "We'll do it immediately," he said, "and then go to Italy. We'll go to Bologna, we'll eat great food. We'll walk around all day and drink grappa at night. We'll observe the world and we'll read the books we never had time for." The woman had not turned around or backed off from the ledge. Beyond her lay the industrial buildings of Long Island City, the endless row houses of Queens. A few clouds moved in the distance. The man shut his eyes and tried to think of how else to change her mind. When he opened them, he saw that between her feet and the ledge was a space, a space that would always exist now between herself and the world. In the long moment when she existed before him for the last time, he thought, How lovely. Then she was gone.

Mark Strand's short short presents the unsuccessful attempt of a stranger to stop the suicide of a woman. The story seems to start at the end. We are witness to her final moments, though we don't know who she is, why she is taking her life, or what is going through her mind as she stands on the roof. The answers to these questions remain a mystery. The woman remains a mystery. We never see her point of view. Instead, the story is seen mostly through the eyes of the stranger, the young man who suddenly appears on the roof, who tries to save her and seduce her at the same time. The all-knowing, or omniscient, narrator, who chooses to see inside the man's mind, nevertheless reveals little about him, only what is relevant to this particular situation. Strand reveals the man's thoughts and feelings through description and dialogue, but shows the woman only through description. For example, we see the action of the wind, which "flattened her skirt against the front of her long thighs." We see her facial expressions: "Her teeth were clenched." We see her gestures: "She lifted her arms. . . ." These details build tension. At the end, the haunting image of the space between the woman's feet and the ledge as she leaves the roof creates a paradox by freezing in time this millisecond. Though the woman is going to her death, the all-knowing narrator says this space will "always" exist in the man's mind: This is the image that will stay with him.

THE HATCHET MAN IN THE LIGHTHOUSE
by William Peden

We are sitting on the trunk of a fallen palmetto pine, Miss Peaches and I, waiting for the sun to set. Far down the beach, where curving strand and sky merge, we can glimpse the pale blue-pink smudge that is Savannah. Below us a few vacationers still linger on the sand, but to the east the shore is deserted; it is almost time to go home to dinner. The moon has not yet risen; the tide is coming in. Out of nowhere a boy jogs toward us, he is neither city-pale nor tidewater-tan; he looks to be between six and seven years old. A few yards from us he slows down, hesitates, finally stops in front of Miss Peaches.

"Hi," she says, and smiles; so do I.

"Hello," he replies, somewhat formally, a city boy, from Savannah perhaps, maybe Beaufort. He is a fine-looking youngster, well formed and with clear blue eyes.

"Been swimming?" I ask, a foolish question, his hair is wet, soaking wet. "How was the water?"

"Yes," he says, and scratches in the sand with his toes. "It was good."

Miss Peaches nods in agreement. "We've been in twice today. The surf was wonderful. Just right."

The boy starts to say something, hesitates, and points across the shining sea toward the mainland. "I've been *there*, too," he announces. "Have you?"

We nod, the boy squints, and points again. "Do you see *it?*"

"See what?" I ask, squinting in turn.

"The Lighthouse." His voice is mildly patronizing. "Way down there. The Lighthouse."

"There's no lighthouse there," I start to say, but Miss Peaches interrupts.

"Yes," she tells the boy. "We see it."

"Have you ever *been* there?"

"No," I say, "no, we've never been there."

"I have." His voice is firm, it brooks no disagreement. "My Mom and Dad took me there."

"Did they?" Miss Peaches asks. "What fun that must have been. What's the lighthouse like?"

He hesitates. "It's big," he says, after a pause. "It's very big."

"Is it," I say. "How big?"

He looks through me and beyond me, his eyes narrowed, scanning the horizon. "It's big enough for him."

"For him?" Miss Peaches and I speak in unison, as though the scene had been rehearsed.

"The hatchet man." His voice is very serious, very earnest. "A giant hatchet man."

"The hatchet man?" I say. "I never knew . . . I mean, what's he like, this hatchet man?"

The boy's clear blue eyes travel from mine, he is seeing something I cannot see.

"He's huge." He gestures with both hands. "He's . . . he's *gargantuan.*"

"Is he!" I suppress a smile, shake my head and glance toward Miss Peaches.

The boy nods emphatically. "There are seahorses out there, too." He extends his arms, embracing the entire expanse of land and slowly-darkening sea. "Man-sized seahorses."

"Yes," Miss Peaches says. "We've seen *them.* But we've never seen the hatchet man. What does he *do* there? What's he *like?*"

Again the boy scratches the sand with his toes. "He's very ugly," he says after a long, thoughtful pause. "He's as ugly as *sin.*" He hesitates, while I bite my lip to suppress a smile. "But he's very . . . very kind."

"Kind?" I say. "That's good to know. I'm glad to know that he's kind. But why . . . why do you call him the hatchet man?"

He looks at me with diminishing patience. "Because that's who he is. Everybody . . ." He slowly shakes his head as if in disbelief. "*Almost* everybody knows that."

Toward Savannah the blue-pink smudge has turned the color of smoke, but in the east a faint glimmer illuminates the water; soon the moon will be rising, there is a slight offshore breeze but there may be some mosquitoes, it is time for us to go back to the house. I extend my hand toward the boy.

"It's very interesting, all these things. Perhaps we'll see you again tomorrow, and you can tell us more about him. We'd like to hear more about the hatchet man . . . and the seahorses, too."

He shakes my hand, he no longer seems irritated at my stupidity. "I'll come back," he says. "I'll come back tomorrow morning."

"Be sure to," Miss Peaches says. "We want to hear more about them."

She leans over and runs her hand lightly through his damp hair. He smiles, heads toward the hard-packed sand at the edge of the sea, and turns and waves to us; we wave back.

"My Mom," he calls, his voice clear and distinct, "My Mom's dead . . . She died yesterday."

We say nothing as he turns again and jogs off, well-coordinated, light on his feet. He will become a good middle-distance runner. Miss Peaches and I watch him, without speaking, until he is only a speck in the distance. I think he stops once to wave, but at that distance and without my glasses I cannot be sure.

A young boy reveals himself unexpectedly, almost as an afterthought, to a couple of strangers he has just met on the beach. Like Chekhov's story, this one is told mostly through dialogue, but it would be difficult to imagine this first-person narrator "overcome with anger" like the narrator in "The Nincompoop." Peden's restrained style is closer to that of Forché in "The Colonel." Unlike the other short shorts so far, you might say this one starts *before* the beginning, because we enter the world of the story before the encounter with the boy. Peden uses setting to draw us in and create the mood when describing, for example, in the distance, " . . . the pale blue-pink smudge that is Savannah." We see clearly where and when the story takes place, but the narrator tells us little about himself and Miss Peaches. He plays a part in the dialogue, but keeps us at a distance, acting mostly as reporter as the action unfolds. Rarely do we see his private thoughts. Near the end, the offhand way in which the boy mentions his mother's death is chilling, as is the silence on the part of the couple, but this understatement, felt also in Forché's story, heightens the shock. The narrator's banal observation that the boy "will become a good middle-distance runner" avoids answering any questions we might have about the boy, his mother, and the impact of his words on the couple. We end up as bystanders to an event that is mysterious, an event we don't fully understand.

CANTON, OHIO: 1956
by Katherine Arnoldi

The shed is next to the house I am supposed to go to. It is the house where a woman sits with a handkerchief to her nose, where a grown-up sleeps with her knees up in the bed next to me, where a boy sleeps in the bed with me. We just came to this house from someplace I do not remember.

At night I sit on the floor, mash soda crackers into a bowl, then lick them out with my tongue. The boy who sleeps in the bed with me puts his head on the floor against a wall, then pushes his legs up and wobbles there, hanging by his heels in the middle of the wallpaper. The grown-up bangs the screen door against the house, gets in a car. The chair where the woman sat opening and closing and folding and tearing a handkerchief is empty. I want to see my eggs, just to look.

There are three eggs. If I pick one up, my hand is sandy inside all day, a special hand.

Behind the house I am supposed to go to is an alley and children play there. They hold to the edges of a blanket, then wave it up and down until someone jumps inside. They fold dolls into cloths, then lay them in cardboard boxes. The boy who sleeps in the bed with me chases boys who have sticks for guns, baseballs, bats.

At night, I see the eggs on the roof falling off.

The woman sitting in the chair with the handkerchief to her nose is not my mother.

The eggs are stuck inside a bowl of twigs and feathers and gum wrappers, and a finger of the roof curls up, brown, around it.

When the girls in the alley notice me, they coo over me, pat my head, then put their fingers on their braids.

The grown-up leads me out onto the back porch and puts me down between her legs on the step in front of her. She rubs oil on my head and tells me her secret.

The sky is white.

I climb the ladder, rest my stomach on the top rung and pet the eggs. I pick them up with two fingers, tuck them into my pocket, and skip to the house to show everybody inside. But someone pulls the pocket open, looks in, puts my arms in the air, pulls my dress off, throws it in the tub, turns on the water. The dress puffs up, blue in the water. I get the pieces of the shell on my finger, put them in my mouth, and swallow them all.

Katherine Arnoldi evokes a little girl's world by describing a number of small events. The events are ordinary, but the world she creates is strange, mysterious. Relationships are hinted at but never made clear. Details, however, are crystal clear, such as, "At night I sit on the floor, mash soda crackers into a bowl, then lick them out with my tongue." But the details don't really add up; only the barest of stories is told. There are recurring figures—the boy who sleeps with her in the bed, the woman with the handkerchief, and the grown-up—but we learn even less about the characters in Arnoldi's story than we did in the previous one. For instance, one character is described like this: "The woman sitting in the chair with the handkerchief to her nose is not my mother." Arnoldi shows what people do rather than who they are. She reveals only gestures, actions. For example, "The grown-up bangs the screen door against the house, gets in a car." Nothing is explained, which is true of Peden's story as well. In his story, we never find out *why* the boy tells them his mother died. Here, however, we don't even know what these actions and events mean. The author doesn't tie the parts neatly together the way she would if she were writing a narrative with a conventional beginning, middle, and end. Instead, she gives us the child's perspective. What we see may be fragments of a lost or half-forgotten reality as an adult remembers herself as a child.

DINNER TIME
by Russell Edson

An old man sitting at a table was waiting for his wife to serve dinner. He heard her beating a pot that had burned her. He hated the sound of a pot when it was beaten, for it advertised its pain in such a way that made him wish to inflict more of the same. And he began to punch at his own face, and his knuckles were red. How he hated red knuckles, that blaring color, more self-important than the wound.

He heard his wife drop the entire dinner on the kitchen floor with a curse. For as she was carrying it in it had burned her thumb. He heard the forks and spoons, the cups and platters all cry at once as they landed on the kitchen floor. How he hated a dinner that, once prepared, begins to burn one to death, and as if that weren't enough, screeches and roars as it lands on the floor, where it belongs anyway.

He punched himself again and fell on the floor.

When he came awake again he was quite angry, and so he punched himself again and felt dizzy. Dizziness made him angry, and so he began to hit his head against the wall, saying, now get real dizzy if you want to get dizzy. He slumped to the floor.

Oh, the legs won't work eh? . . . He began to punch his legs. He had taught his head a lesson and now he would teach his legs a lesson.

Meanwhile he heard his wife smashing the remaining dinnerware and the dinnerware roaring and shrieking.

He saw himself in the mirror on the wall. Oh, mock me, will you. And so he smashed the mirror with a chair, which broke. Oh, don't want to be a chair no more; too good to be sat on, eh? He began to beat the pieces of the chair.

He heard his wife beating the stove with an ax. He called, when're we going to eat? as he stuffed a candle into his mouth.

When I'm good and ready, she screamed.

Want me to punch your bun? he screamed.

Come near me and I'll kick an eye out of your head.

I'll cut your ears off.

I'll give you a slap right in the face.

I'll kick you right in the breadbasket.

I'll break you in half.

The old man finally ate one of his hands. The old woman said, damn fool, whyn't you cook it first? You go on like a beast—you know I have to subdue the kitchen every night, otherwise it'll cook me and serve me to the mice on my best china. And you know what small eaters they are; next would come the flies, and how I hate flies in my kitchen.

The old man swallowed a spoon. Okay, said the old woman, now we're short one spoon.

The old man, growing angry, swallowed himself.

Okay, said the woman, now you've done it.

An event as commonplace as dinner becomes, in the hands of Russell Edson, an extraordinary event. Here, the fantastic arises out of the ordinary. The impossible seems possible. We suspend judgment because the narrator's voice has the authority of truth, even though we know that in any context other than the story's, inanimate objects can't behave like people: "the forks and spoons, the cups and platters" can't all cry at once, for example, and an old man can't swallow himself, though he might conceivably hurt himself in other ways described. He might "punch at his own face," for instance, or he and his wife might behave violently toward objects, but the objects in a realistic story would not react. Edson's details are drawn as precisely as those in a realistic story, but the violence is tempered by humor. The old woman, for example, complains to her husband that she must "subdue the kitchen every night, otherwise it'll cook me and serve me to the mice on my best china. And you know what small eaters they are; next would come the flies, and how I hate flies in my kitchen." These carefully observed details are proof that the world he portrays is true or, if not true, at least possible. This is how the story *would* happen if it *could* happen because there is a logic here. Edson has set the fantastic *within* a world we recognize, a world that is still familiar though it is skewed.

WAITING
by Josephine Foo

"I don't know what you mean," Catherine said. "I would go anywhere in the world with you, even to Istanbul."

Ned glanced at her with a glazed expression. "Paris is far enough," he breathed, lying prone on Catherine's purple silk sheets while Catherine's head bobbed at the edges of his view. Catherine stood up and went to the kitchen to get a refill of wine for herself. She returned, swaying, and stood in the doorway. "You're so beautiful, Ned. You're beautiful."

Ned focused his eyes on her, thinking of all the other times Catherine, drunk, swayed in doorways with her dress in disarray and her face smudged and sorrowful.

He opened his arms and Catherine fell into them, sighing. "Kiss me," she whispered. He pressed his lips to Catherine's forehead, her temples and the shells of her ears. He ran languid and cool fingers through Catherine's tussled dark hair and felt on his flattened wrists her earrings's hanging stones. "Kiss me," Catherine said, beads of sweat forming on her face. "My lips, Ned. Lips."

Ned pushed her away, turned over on his side away from her and looked out the window at the East River and a barge which just then sailed into view, towing a block of garbage bound down river to Staten Island. The red-ringed industrial chimneys of Queens billowed white smoke. Clouds of gray strolled along the sky. Ned wondered what it would be like to be a cloud going for a walk around the world. Of course it dissipated and became rain, falling on soil or concrete. But then it renewed itself and continued, persisted, and stepped on no toes. An image from the past came to mind, that of a young boy tying the shoelaces of his father, too fat to bend over. Ned remembered Catherine's large feet moving in a fiery flamenco dance to the tragic summary of a twelve string guitar. Her feet stamped down loudly on the tile floor. Her red lit-up face offered to the crowds with a passion that was so hungry it compelled all to consume her. The fringes of her many-layered skirt encircled her turning shape like a boomerang riding the parameters of a field. Her ample arms thrown up and her fingers splayed suggested flowers. He, a waiter then, had stood watching in the shadows, off to the side, unobtrusively. Tray in hand, he would soon go round, cleaning the tables.

He bent low out of jealousy and spilled nothing, out of fear, as Catherine entranced everyone.

"Catherine," Ned said, reaching out to her soft shape and pulling her close. Their smells mingled; their bodies grew fluid and warm. They rolled around the queen size bed, struggling for intimacy, then lay huddled together silent.

Soon, Catherine lifted her heavy body up. There was the sound of shower water. Catherine liked long, long very hot showers. Ned picked up a magazine and started to read.

He closed his eyes and sat, waiting. For swirling fringes. A patient man, he read his magazine slowly and carefully.

Catherine emerged from the shower sobered up by the steam. She went over to the bar and poured a glass. Then giving a low cynical laugh, she retreated into her bedroom.

"What's wrong?" Ned said, bewildered. "Why do you drink so much?"

He went over to Catherine and helped her zip up her dress.

"Why am I not helping you? Why can't we just be happy?"

Catherine put her hand on his cheek and whispered gently, "You sweet and simple thing." Ned fell back as if she had hit him. He went to the door and said, "I'm going for a walk."

"Don't," Catherine said.

Ned shrugged, shutting the door.

Catherine picked up a cigarette from an antique gold case. Now that the room was free of Ned's presence, she felt at peace. With steady hands, she smoked in silence, leaning on one foot, cradling one arm. Once finished, her fingers, free, searched for another. She looked outside at the view of billowing clouds and at the tidal river sloshing waves up the embankment, wondering at her excessive temerity in dealing with matters of truth.

Some weeks ago, she had begun to find Ned's lips repugnant. Rather than admit that to him, she had grown more needy. Rather than explain to Ned that she no longer loved him, she had become grasping and panic-stricken. Catherine picked up yet another glass of wine and sank her soul in it.

Where was Ned? This waiting, she felt, as the liquid hit the bottom of her belly, would kill her.

A woman who is no longer in love is afraid to let go of her lover in this short short by Josephine Foo. After reading this story, one of my students said it didn't feel like a short short because the reader learns so much about the characters. The story focuses on a moment in Ned and Catherine's relationship, but because the characters are drawn with such rich, vivid details and are shown in the past as well as the present, and from more than one point of view, they seem more developed than other characters in short shorts. For example, Ned remembers Catherine doing a flamenco dance: "The fringes of her many-layered skirt encircled her turning shape like a boomerang riding the parameters of a field." The omniscient narrator describes Ned as a waiter, cleaning tables: "He bent low out of jealousy and spilled nothing, out of fear, as Catherine entranced everyone." They are individuals, not symbols, though events are compressed. Take this description of sex, for instance: "Their smells mingled; their bodies grew fluid and warm. They rolled around the queen size bed, struggling for intimacy. . . ." The story is told by an all-knowing narrator who slips in and out of each character's mind with relative ease. This is no small feat in a short short, where a shifting point of view may seem confusing or abrupt. At first, we see Catherine through Ned's eyes. When he leaves, the point of view shifts to Catherine and allows us to see that what frightens her is *not* wanting Ned. Writers are often told to *show* rather than *tell*, but in this instance, the explanation of Catherine's neediness, arising from her fear, sets up the end and holds the punch.

MY SISTER AND THE QUEEN OF ENGLAND
by Lydia Davis

For fifty years, nag nag nag, and harp harp harp. No matter what my sister did, it wasn't good enough for my mother, or for my father either. She moved to England to get away, and married an Englishman, and when he died she married another Englishman, but that wasn't enough.

Then my sister was awarded the Order of the British Empire. My parents flew over to England for the ceremony, and watched from across the ballroom floor as my sister walked out there alone and stood and talked to the Queen of England, and they were impressed. My mother told me in a letter that no one else in the line of people receiving honors that day stopped to talk so long to the Queen as my sister did. I wasn't surprised, because my sister has always been a great talker, no matter what the occasion. But when I asked my mother later what my sister was wearing she didn't remember very well—some kind of a tent, she said. And she said my sister spent all morning trying to get some white gloves. But then she told me that everyone loved my sister, and everyone praised her. Four Lords of Parliament had mentioned her in their maiden speeches because of what she had done for the disabled, and she treated the disabled, my mother said, like anyone else, and she talked to her drivers the same way she talked to the Lords and the disabled, and no one minded the way her house looked though it was worse than ever. She said the house looked worse than ever, and my sister was still letting her figure go, she wouldn't stop talking, and she still drank too much, and did it where no one could see her, but they felt they had to keep quiet, she told me, because who were they, now, to say anything against her, who had done so much good, and who was so admired. So I'm proud of my sister, I'm happy for her because of the award, but I'm also happy that my mother and father have finally been silenced for a while, and will let her alone for a while, though I don't think it will be for long, and I'm sorry it took the Queen of England to do it.

It takes the presentation of an award to stop the narrator's parents from criticizing her sister, at least "for a while." In contrast to Foo's rich, vivid imagery in "Waiting," Davis' writing is spare. Notice the compressed language she uses to sum up the way the narrator's parents treat her sister: "For fifty years, nag nag nag, and harp harp harp." Unlike the other short shorts in this chapter, we hear about the main event secondhand, since the narrator wasn't there to witness it. We are removed from the award ceremony and its details. The real subject is the narrator. What fuels the story is her anger, even when her stance is reporter-like, and she tells *without comment* what her mother said about her sister and the ceremony. Notice how the narrator repeats the words "worse than ever" when referring to the way her mother describes her sister's house. This repetition subtly emphasizes the daughter's disapproval of her mother's words. The story reveals less about the sister abroad—whose actions take place at a time other than the time of the story—than it does about the narrator, whose interpretation is the key.

THREE

A COMPARISON WITH LONGER STORIES

Think of this chapter as your orientation to the short short form. In the next pages, I will show you what makes short shorts different from longer stories and what qualities they have in common. I will set some boundaries. These are probably not the only boundaries that can be set for the short short, but they will give you a sense of the form.

This chapter has little to do with *how* you will write these little stories. That will be addressed in chapters four and five. Here, I will discuss the basics.

WHAT IS A STORY?

The following definition applies to stories of several thousand words as well as to those of several hundred words or less. A story is a container for change. It's a container in which something happens. That something needs to create an experience for the reader. The reader needs to be moved. What happens in the story need not be extreme, but by the end, something needs to have shifted. The shift may be in the mind of a character, such as the husband who realizes he was wrong to suspect his wife of cheating. Or the shift may be shown by a physical action, such as the girl running away from the home she hates.

The story can be an incident, an episode, an anecdote, a fable, a parable, a fantasy, a monologue, or a fiction disguised as an essay. A story can simply present a change in a character's state of mind or point of view. The change may be a realization, a revelation, an epiphany, an understanding, or a decision. It might result in finding a lost dog, nursing a sick man back to health, falling in love for the first time, or deciding to sell a house.

WHAT IS A SHORT SHORT STORY?

In *Short Shorts, An Anthology of the Shortest Stories*, critic Irving Howe said that short short stories are like short stories, "only more so." He means that the short short is such an extreme version of the short story that it becomes a separate genre. But not all fiction under a thousand words (the limit in this section of the book) fits that criterion. The fact that short shorts have fewer words than other stories doesn't necessarily make them *extreme*. Distinctions between this brief form and longer stories are less than clear-cut.

The short short story has been defined in a number of ways. One of my favorite definitions was coined by Howe in his anthology when he spoke of this concise form of writing "as a moment rendered in its wink of immediacy." Another definition I like was made by William Peden in *Sudden Fiction*, another anthology of short shorts. He described one as "the opening or closing of a window, a moment of insight." In that same anthology, writer Russell Banks said these little stories "leave the reader anxious in a particularly satisfying way." I would like to add to these definitions one of my own: A short short is a story that gets quickly to the core and reveals the essence of a situation or moment in very few words. It is complete in itself and may express as many moods and take as many forms as longer stories. It may be a snapshot or a single frame, but there's great freedom within its small boundaries.

The short short is a relative of the poem. This hybrid form lies somewhere between fiction and poetry and owes a debt to the prose poem. In fact, it is sometimes difficult or even impossible to distinguish a *narrative* prose poem from a short short since the former also tells a story. For example, "The Colonel," by Carolyn Forché, which we discussed in chapter two, has been defined both ways. Each of these forms results from a process of free association. Both may use language that is musical. Both may be dense or compact. Prose poems, however, are not bound by the basic fictional elements discussed below.

THE BASIC ELEMENTS

The short short and the longer story share certain basic elements, some of which function differently in the short form than they do in the longer story. These elements are

- characters
- setting and mood
- point of view
- situation and plot
- style and voice

In any story, one or more of these elements may be emphasized.

Characters

Short shorts and longer stories have characters. Whether they are human, animal, or inanimate objects that behave like human beings, as is the case when "the forks and spoons, the cups and platters all cry at once" in Russell Edson's "Dinner Time" (see chapter two), it is often—but not always—characters who precipitate the change in a story.

Characters—who may be revealed through action, description, or speech—function differently in short shorts than they do in longer fictions. A longer story allows for some development of the characters over time; the short short does not. In the latter, you see the characters in a momentary flash. You see them in a key episode, in a climactic moment. Take the boy in William Peden's story "The Hatchet Man in the Lighthouse" (see chapter two) who, as he is walking away, tells the couple he has just met that his mom died yesterday. Characters in short shorts may be in the middle of some physical activity, such as driving, cooking, or taking long walks like several of Robert Walser's characters; they may be in the process of making decisions; or they may realize something for the first time. In most cases, you see them neither before nor after these moments or particular situations.

Characters may or may not operate as individuals in short shorts. Some *stand for* a particular way of being or a particular attitude or state of mind. For example, the wife in Robert Walser's story "Nothing At All" (see chapter two) is a portrait of indecisiveness. We know nothing else about her. She is a symbol. A character who functions only as a symbol is known only in relation to whatever she represents. But even though you, as reader, don't know the character as an individual, you will identify with the situation. In so doing, you will have sympathy (even if that character is not realistically drawn) simply because the character is *representative* of a situation that strikes a universal chord.

The governess in Chekhov's "The Nincompoop" (scc chapter two) is the epitome of powerlessness, but she is also a character in her own right: She is realistically portrayed. Though we see her only in the exchange with her employer, we may deduce other things about her life through their exchange. For example, we may infer that she is cheated in other situations, by dressmakers, butchers, bakers, and so on. In other words, you may infer who characters are through their actions, thoughts, or emotions at a given time. You may glimpse their essence without knowing them.

Some characters, such as Catherine in Josephine Foo's "Waiting" (see chapter two), feel more developed because a few well-chosen details show them in the past. In Catherine's case, these details, seen mostly through Ned's eyes, function as background and give a sense of history. In other words, a few significant details pass for development in a short short and may create a specific character who is larger than the story. We see more about her than is said.

Setting and Mood

Both the longer story and the short short happen in a particular place. The setting, as it is called, may serve as backdrop, or it may be the subject if, for instance, a story presents the aftermath of a tornado on a small town. In a short short, the setting may be rendered in very few words, such as "It happened on the beach" or "He was walking across the street when . . ."

The "mood" refers to the atmosphere or tone. It creates in the reader the feeling of "being there" by giving sensory information: The reader can smell the damp forest, taste the freshly baked bread, feel the softness of silk against skin. Mood may be suggested by setting. A story that takes place on a dark city street late at night has a different atmosphere from a story that takes place in daylight on a prairie filled with wildflowers. The mood may also be suggested by the characters. The man sitting with his head in his hands evokes a different feeling in the reader than the little girl who can hardly contain her excitement as she rips the wrappings off her birthday present.

In general, mood has more weight in a short short than it has in a longer story because in a short short, you don't have the space or time to develop characters or theme. These little stories rely upon an instantaneous recognition for effect.

Point of View

The point of view is the angle or perspective from which a narrative is told. This angle determines what is emphasized and what is kept in the background. Point of view answers these two questions: Who is telling the short short? How does the narrator feel about the story? The point of view may be personal or impersonal.

All stories, long or short, have points of view. In fact, you can say that the point of view creates the story. If, for example, the narrator is telling about a lover who jilted him, he will see his former lover in a different light than will her fiancé just before their wedding. The same character may be seen from a variety of viewpoints. Each can be used to create an entirely different story or short short. The point of view can shift within a story from one character to another. This is much less likely to happen in a short short because it is so brief, but it does happen in "Waiting." The story is seen through Ned's eyes until the second-to-last paragraph when the reader sees it from Catherine's point of view.

First Person A story or short short may be told in first-person singular, meaning the events are seen by only one character. First person is the angle many beginning writers use. *I* may be an autobiographical point of view, or it may be a point of view that has little or nothing to do with the writer.

First person gives a story an immediacy and makes the reader easily identify with the narrator, because a real person seems to be telling the story. A character can reveal things about himself in first person that the third-person narrator couldn't know, as in "The Nincompoop."

Third Person The third-person narrator—*he, she,* or *it*—sees the story from a distance. The narrator can act as reporter and relate events objectively, with an emotional detachment the characters inside the story could never possess. In this instance, the narrator is a neutral witness, an observer. The story is told in an indifferent factual way. The narrator shows things and their positions, action, and dialogue but never says what they mean.

Or the narrator may serve as interpreter. *He, she*, or *it* can comment from a position *outside* the story on events and characters *inside* the story. (See Lydia Davis' "My Sister and the Queen of England" in chapter two.) The narrator can't get inside the characters' minds, but the narrator can make available to the reader insights about the characters that they may hardly know about themselves.

The Unnamed All-Knowing Narrator An unnamed third-person, all-knowing narrator has the authority of God, knows all sides of a situation, and is able to see inside the characters' minds. (See, for example, Josephine Foo's story in chapter two.) This narrator knows more than the characters know. In a story told by an omniscient narrator, simultaneous events or incidents in different parts of the world may be described.

Second Person and First-Person Plural The infrequently used second person *you* usually refers to the reader. But in Don Shea's story "Blindsided" (see chapter two), *you* seems to refer to the narrator. In this case, the narrator "objectifies" his own experience: He uses *you* to create distance from himself, to stand back and observe his own reactions to the man in the subway, when he says, for example, "and then you recognized the song." At the same time, *you* tends to draw the reader into the narrative and makes the reader part of it.

You can also be a kind of one-sided conversation when it addresses a subject in second person that would usually be described in third. The first-person plural *we* is also used infrequently. It may seem evasive: Who is *we*? Or it may be mysterious.

Situation and Plot

Plot In longer stories, the plot or story line can develop over time. But in a short short, there is no development or, at most, the merest hint of it. The narrator may suggest the past or future, but in general, only the time of the story matters. Even in short shorts that span a number of years, events are compact.

In the short short when we speak of plot, we are speaking about situation, or a particular set of circumstances happening at a certain point in time. The short short happens in a flash. The story doesn't have time to *go* somewhere. It is already there happening when we see it. The traditional beginning, middle, and end may be absent, replaced instead by the moment.

Simply by virtue of its length, longer fiction is more likely than the short short to embrace more than one situation or story line. Usually, the situation in a short short is simple: The writer needs only to go from point A to point B. But, to hold the reader's interest, the writer of longer works needs to keep the story moving.

Structure When we talk about the structure of a piece of fiction, we are talking about shape: the plan, the design. It is more difficult to hold in mind the shape of the longer form simply because of its length. When I think of shape in a short short, I think of a piece of architecture. I imagine the skeleton of a building in which every steel beam is in place. If any of the beams is missing, the structure becomes unsteady and is likely to fall.

The Arc Both the short short and the longer story have a high point, or arc. This is the moment the reader has been waiting for, the decisive action or change. The story hinges on this action. This is the moment when the volcano erupts, the young man decides to join the navy, or the girl turns on her heels and walks away.

The Point Both kinds of stories need to show us something about our world or something about ourselves. They need not have a "message" or "moral." But they do need to reach a conclusion or provide some insight into a situation. The insight may be nothing more illuminating than the narrator's conviction that the situation recounted cannot be understood or that the problem at hand is unsolvable.

The theme may be neatly tied up at the end. This is the case in "The Nincompoop" when the narrator sums up the story by saying, "How easy it is to be strong in this world!" But the point doesn't have to be directly stated. More often, it's implied, especially in the short short, where brevity is important. Let's say you are moved to write about how badly some parents treat their children. This is a broad topic. To make this point, you need to create a specific situation in which you *show* exactly how the children in a particular family are abused. In other words, to create an experience for the reader, you *show* instead of *tell*.

In a longer narrative, you have some time to make your point, so a theme may be developed, but as I said, there is little or no development in a short short. The theme is revealed in an instant. The theme is *the heart* of the story, but it may be too subtle to see at first. You may need to reread a piece several times before you "get it." In your own exercises, you may have to "dig" for it. When you find *the heart*, you've found the key to your short short. Revising is often the act of uncovering it. It may lie hidden like buried treasure in your words.

Some writers set out intentionally to explore particular themes or subjects. Others do not. "It's just a story," one of this school will say. These writers don't start with a purpose: The story may be nothing more than a vague feeling when they begin.

Style and Voice

Style is *how* the writer tells the tale: the words the writer chooses, the phrases, the kinds of sentences preferred; whether they are short and succinct, or long and complex. The style is the writer's "voice" inside her head. She may, in fact, have many voices, reflecting different feelings, moods, and states of mind. Those voices may be heard in the variety of characters the writer creates.

THE THREE UNIQUE QUALITIES OF SHORT SHORTS

The three unique qualities of short short stories are brevity, intensity, and surprise. Most, however, share other qualities, too. These secondary qualities—compression, indirection, immediacy, a single focus, tightness, and precision—cannot to my mind be divorced from the three unique qualities. Not every short short has all these qualities, but each has some. These secondary qualities will also be discussed here.

Brevity

This first one is obvious. Short short stories are brief, but exactly *how* brief is a matter of conjecture. There is no agreed upon length that defines the form. In this section of the book, stories will range from approximately a hundred to a thousand words.

When you work on such an intimate scale, every word you use is magnified. Every word assumes a weight, an importance it probably would not have among five thousand others. One misused word among thousands will probably not change the meaning of your story unless the word misused is critically positioned, but one misused word in a story of one hundred, five hundred, or seven hundred words can throw everything off balance. In a short short, every word counts double.

Because of this, each one needs to be chosen with the utmost care.

In these little stories, superfluous and elaborate words are removed. The ones that remain may be pared down still further. Words are chosen *to nail* ideas, places, and characters. They are used to reveal the essence of a moment or situation, so they need to be exact. Some stories are compressed into the smallest possible space. Often there are few descriptive adjectives and adverbs and yet we see the scene perfectly. A short short is told in such a way that the reader knows more than what is being said. Information is suggested rather than "spelled out." In other words, we see more than the words say.

Poetic Language To ensure brevity, short shorts demand greater use of poetic language, words and phrases that connect disparate things, people, and events in original and ingenious ways. This language may be called metaphorical. When one thing is spoken of in terms of another, a metaphor is created. The connection of two things by means of *like* or *as* is referred to as a simile. An analogy may be said to compare things that are similar. Metaphors and similes are used, particularly in poetry, to make connections that literal description cannot make. Their use, however, is not limited to poetry.

Consider the poetic language in American poet Robert Kelly's one-page story "Rosary." In it, a man carrying rosary beads at night down a deserted country road admires a woman with "glossy black hair" he sees through the window of a building. Midway in the story, the narrator says the woman may have seen him coming and mistaken his crystal beads for a gleaming dagger. Here's the story's pivotal sentence.

> It may be that she longed for this silent shadowy assassin
> to come destroy her, to rescue her from hard work or loneliness
> or her glossy hair.

In this surprising sentence, the narrator refers to the woman's glossy hair as though it were a burden like hard work or an affliction like loneliness from which she might seek the relief of death.

Consider the poetic use of language in Richard Brautigan's surprising short short "The Weather in San Francisco," in which a very old woman goes to a butcher to buy liver on a sunless afternoon. The butcher tries to persuade her to buy hamburger instead, but she holds her ground. The narrator observes the woman as she leaves the shop.

> By using her bones like the sails of a ship, the old woman
> passed outside into the street.

At the magical end of the story, we learn she bought the liver for her
bees.

> The bees came to her and gathered about her lovingly while
> she unwrapped the liver and placed it upon a cloudy silver
> platter that soon changed into a sunny day.

In this image of the "cloudy silver platter" that becomes "a sunny
day," the reader sees the old woman's world transformed.

Intensity

Intensity is intrinsic to the short short form. It brings the story into
existence. The story is born out of a need. There is an urgency behind
the words, a deeply felt emotion that prompts a writer to create. It
is unconscious energy made conscious, flowing through the writer's
fingers. Intensity is the energy that is there in the story from the start.

Longer stories may be intense, but words occupy a smaller space
in a short short. Sometimes words seem on the verge of breaking out.
They strain against the walls of the narrative. Imagine a balloon filled
with so much helium it seems ready to burst.

Intensity may be heightened not only by compression, but also by
a fast pulsing rhythm, by repetition, or by the depiction of an extreme
situation or event. Consider the beginning of one of French writer
Nathalie Sarraute's "Tropisms," in which the physical details are extreme. This is from her book of the same name.

> She was sitting crouched on a corner of her chair, squirming,
> her neck outstretched, her eyes bulging: "Yes, yes, yes, yes,"
> she said, and she confirmed each part of the sentence with a
> jerk of her head.

In most short shorts, the intensity is not quite so apparent. As readers,
we experience it more subtly. Sometimes the form may be likened to
a cooking pot with a tightly closed lid. As readers, we see only the
closed pot at first. But when we look closely we notice the lid vibrating
slightly but insistently, which shows that whatever is inside—in this
case the content of the story—is pressing against the lid, threatening

to blow it off. The short short may appear calm and quiet on the surface, but we feel the urgency behind it.

Or it may happen that a story starts quietly and builds. The intensity may be found in the accumulation of words. Words have weight, more weight at the end than at the beginning. Or it may be that the writer has saved the intensity for an epiphany or revelation at the final moment. In any case, ordinary prose seems thin or sluggish when compared with the contained energy in short shorts. This intensity or urgency keeps this form of fiction from sounding like an outline or summary.

You won't, however, have to worry about creating intensity. It will happen in your exercises as you tap your unconscious. The more *emotionally charged* the material, the more urgent or intense your writing will be. Whereas in a longer story, the intensity may diminish over a number of pages, the form of the short short keeps it intact.

Surprise or Unexpectedness

When a short short is surprising or unexpected, it catches the reader off guard. The reader may think a story is going in one direction when in fact, it's really going in another. The surprise provides a jolt.

The surprise cannot always be pinpointed in a particular part of a story. It may be the subject matter, the voice, or the tone of the piece. It may be what doesn't happen or what isn't said.

In a story, the reader is drawn in by physical details, which create a dream in the reader's mind. He no longer sees words on the page and, instead, is swept along by the story. In the longer tale, the reader has at least some time to spend in the fictional world. In the short short, however, that world ends almost as soon as it begins. The short short accomplishes its goals in one broad sweep. The reader is seduced, then abandoned, but not without getting an insight of some sort.

What is left out is as important as what is said. You see parts of the story out of the corner of your eye. You can *infer* certain ideas about characters or situations that are not directly stated. These things happen backstage or under the surface. You may compare a short short to a tree. You see the trunk, leaves, and branches growing above the earth. What you don't see is the system of roots beneath the soil, but you know the roots are there because the tree could not otherwise exist.

How is the surprise in a short short made known? Often, the story *twists*. The twist signals or reveals an abrupt change of perspective or turn of events. This may happen in the middle or at the end. It wrenches the story from its mooring and relocates it. It may change the story's direction or distort the meaning of what we have come to know so far.

The twist may be in the form of a comment that seems inevitable once it is made, though you would never have thought of it otherwise. However off-putting, the surprise must fit into the existing logic of the story. It is something seen from an odd angle or perspective, for example. It does not necessarily bring in something new, such as a new idea, but more often shows us a different side of what we already know, a side we wouldn't ordinarily see in a particular situation without the writer's help.

In "Gelman," a very short essay-like story, which has the feel of an experience drawn from real life, Uruguayan writer Eduardo Galeano tells us about an Argentine poet whose children were kidnapped and tortured; one was finally murdered by the Argentine military. He ends the story with these unexpected lines.

> And I've wondered: if God exists, why does he just walk on
> by? Could God be an atheist?

In another essay-like story by Galeano called "The Language of Art," a poor Cuban refugee named Chinolope happens to be on the street in New York with a camera someone gave him when the gangster Albert Anastasia is shot down in a barbershop. Chinolope's photograph of this event makes him rich. Here's the story's end.

> Chinolope had managed to photograph death. Death was
> there: not in the dead man, nor in the killer. Death was in the
> face of the barber looking on.

The twist changes the shape of the story by deviating from the expected plan or design. When there are several twists in a story, as there are in Luisa Valenzuela's "Vision Out of the Corner of One Eye" in chapter two, the shape keeps changing. In the beginning, for example, when the narrator in the bus says a man "put his hand" on her behind but "crossed himself" when they passed a church, the last thing you expect the narrator to say is, "He's a good sort after all. . . ."

Whenever the story begins to look predictable, the narrator says or does something surprising, which keeps the reader off balance.

Surprise endings or unexpected twists sometimes happen effortlessly in the short short. They are part of the particular logic of the unconscious. The more you allow the unexpected to happen in your exercises, the more likely you are to see these twists take place without trying, though it will not always be that easy.

You may need to juggle your conscious and unconscious mind. This means going back and forth between intuition and logic until you find a twist that works. How do you know if it works? Once again, it *feels* right.

FOUR BASIC KINDS OF SHORT SHORTS

I have divided short shorts roughly into four categories: single incidents, stories that compress time, stories that reveal a mind, and stories that defy ordinary reality. This doesn't mean that all short shorts fall comfortably inside these boundaries. Some are at home in more than one category. You may find some that fall into none. These categories are not meant to be straitjackets. Think of them instead as various doorways through which you may approach the short short.

Single Incidents

Most short shorts focus on single incidents. These incidents may be moments of discovery or realization, climactic moments, key episodes, and epiphanies. They are easily grasped by the reader and happen in a brief time span.

In general, plots are not as complicated as they may be in longer stories. As stated earlier, there is a progression only from point A to point B. Longer stories may also focus on single incidents, but the focus in the short short is likely to be sharper, more pronounced, and the story more energetic or intense. There is little room for recounting more than the event. Everything or almost everything else has been stripped away. There is none of the exposition or digressions you may find in longer works.

For instance, the writer of a longer piece may choose to indulge in elaborate descriptions of setting. In the short short, however, such descriptions are superfluous unless *directly* linked to the incident at hand. The incident is all we see, and we see it in a momentary flash.

Often, we don't know what happened before the incident and we don't know what happened afterward, though we may be able to *infer* things not directly stated. In any case, the incident needs to be engaging enough so we are satisfied with what we have.

In "A Full Afternoon," Brazilian writer Clarice Lispector tells the story of a woman riding a bus beside a man with a monkey. The monkey, vividly described in the story, is a creature of interest and enchantment not only to the woman but to the entire bus. At one point, the narrator says, the monkey jumped onto the woman's lap and she reacted with

> . . . the shy pleasure of one who is chosen.

This occurred a little later on the bus.

> . . . one woman told another that she had a cat. Whoever loved something told about it.

In this happy atmosphere, a collision between the bus and a truck takes place, causing everyone to flee. The woman forgets about the monkey until she is safely in a cab. Then she is sorry that "events had been distributed so badly" that meeting the monkey and a near calamity should have happened simultaneously. The narrator goes on to say that after this incident, the woman, whose life was usually dull, didn't expect any excitement for quite a while, though it turns out that other things happened to her on that day as well. The story ends with this line.

> In any case, it was an afternoon of fluttering banners.

In this image, and in an earlier image of the bus moving forward through a breeze "as if fluttering with banners," there's a sense of movement, of excitement, of celebration perhaps. A single incident may be enough to give you a vivid picture of a character's life.

Stories That Compress Time
The form of the short short is closer to the poem, but the content is closer to the novel. In the anthology *Sudden Fiction*, Mark Strand said the short short "can do in a page what the novel does in two hundred." In a page or two, it can tell a story that extends over a period of years, without making us feel as though we are missing something. How

does it accomplish this? Through compression. Significant details represent particular moments that stand out in the passage of time.

Take, for instance, a story in which a woman named Mindy marries a guy named Al who ends up leaving her for a younger woman. Let's say the story starts five years earlier when Mindy meets Al at a party. What is significant about their meeting? The fact that Mindy snubs Al because he's a poor artist. She likes only rich, successful men. By the time she meets Al again, however, four years later, he's a well-known painter. Since this story is about their relationship rather than the rise of his career, a couple of sentences about his career will probably suffice. These lines might read, "In the four years since they had met, Al had become a successful painter. His last gallery show had sold out." Those are significant details because once they are established, the reader understands *why* Mindy accepts a date with Al four years later. In other words, the reader doesn't need to know details about his life or career that don't have any direct relation to the couple's eventual marriage and divorce.

Stories that compress time are pared down—I like to think of them as sculpted—until only what's essential remains. As in other kinds of short shorts, more information is implied than stated.

In the short short, there is no time but the moment, or a series of moments, each represented by a telling detail or two. Everything that happens is swept along toward a finale, which may not be a finale at all. Short shorts can begin and end in the middle of things. They can seem as though they have been lifted out of life or separated from the stream of things so that we may look at them exclusively.

Ernest Hemingway's "A Very Short Story" begins in Italy during the war when a wounded American soldier and an American nurse fall in love, and ends long after the war is over. With an economy of language, we are told about the soldier's affair with the nurse, named Luz, in the same sentence that we learn about his recovery. Both the affair and his recovery are implied rather than stated by the narrator.

> After he got on crutches he used to take the temperatures
> so that Luz would not have to get up from the bed.

The phrase "so that Luz would not have to get up from the bed" suggests the affair without actually saying it.

The couple want to marry but are forced to wait because of the war. When the war ends, he wants her to return home with him, but she wants to wait until he's settled. They quarrel. After he leaves, their quarrel not over, she has an affair with an Italian army major and writes to the ex-soldier in America, saying that she will marry the major. In her letter, she also says

> . . . theirs had only been a girl and boy affair.

But the marriage never takes place and the ex-soldier never replies to her letter. He does, however, get gonorrhea in Chicago. At the conclusion, which is open-ended, the reader is left with the feeling that life goes on, not always happily.

What we learn about the characters in this story concerns only their love affair. We know nothing about the nurse or the soldier before they met. We never find out what happened to him after he contracted gonorrhea, nor do we find out what became of the nurse. Nevertheless, the story *feels* complete.

In general, a short short feels complete when the questions raised by the story are answered. The trick is knowing exactly *which* questions to raise. You may narrow it down by eliminating questions that don't directly relate to *the heart* of the story.

Stories That Reveal a Mind

In stories that reveal a mind, a narrator presents a monologue or flow of memories. In the monologue, the narrator may, for example, recount a single incident, but here the incident is secondary. In this kind of story, voice is everything. You may be more engaged by the way the story is told, the manner of its telling, than you are by the story itself. You may be intrigued by the writer's choice of words, unusual word plays, metaphors, and analogies. You may be intrigued by the writer's insights and point of view. Your interest centers on *the way the narrator sees the world*.

Robert Walser, who was a precursor of Franz Kafka, wrote many stories of this kind. In his stories, the narrator's thoughts, ruminations, and odd interpretations interest and surprise the reader. His short shorts are not essentially different from his longer stories—the same voice enlivens each of them—and yet, the short shorts feel more concentrated, focused, and intense. In the sly tale called "The Maid," which is part of "Two Strange Stories," the narrator tells the story of a maid who is distraught when the child she loves, the child of her rich employer, gets lost. The maid looks for her all over the world, "even in Persia," where she asks the light in a "broad dark tower" where her child is. Before it goes out, the light tells her to "go on looking for another ten years." The maid does as she is told. She looked

> in all the parts and on all the bypaths of the earth, even in France. In France there is a great and splendid city called Paris, and to this city she came.

In Paris she suddenly finds the child in a garden.

> She saw it and died of joy. Why did she die? Did that do her any good? Yet she was old now and could not endure so much any more. The child is now a grand and beautiful lady. If you should ever meet her, give her my best regards.

Without Robert Walser's voice, this little story would read like a summary or a sketch instead of a mock fable. It is not the story of the maid's travels to find the lost child that engages us so much as it is the voice of the narrator, which is detached and mocking, but at the same time compassionate. In this short short, a mind is revealed more than a story told.

Stories That Defy Ordinary Reality

This category includes stories that explore the strange, the spooky, the fantastic. The things that happen in these stories defy the laws of reality as we know them. Brautigan's "The Weather in San Francisco," which ends mysteriously with the old woman's "cloudy silver platter" turning into "a sunny day" is a poetic example in this category. In this type, the reader is asked to suspend disbelief. To do so, the reader must be sufficiently intrigued or impressed by the narration to give up obvious objections to what she knows is not true. The writer's premise may be impossible, but he establishes credibility by using realistic details. Within the context or framework established by the writer, the story makes sense. There is a logic to what happens. The reader can say it is poetically true. Consider Barry Yourgrau's opening sentences in his story "Milk."

> On a bet, a man climbs inside a cow. Once there he decides
> to stay.

He tells us what it's like to be inside the cow, but at the same time, he hangs on to a shred of the real world when he says he can still hear his friends' cries of disapproval "from the world of sanity and reality." This realistic detail makes the story believable on its own terms. The "real" world doesn't totally disappear until the man inside the cow plugs up his ears with the cow's "milky stomach mucus." At the surprise ending, however, the point of view shifts from the man to the cow.

> Her large, sensitive eyes brim with concern as she tries to
> fathom her new fate and responsibility.

The critic Irving Howe wrote that the short short "accepts the enigmas of confinement and . . . strives for a rapid unity of impression." This "rapid unity" is possible because the beginning is never far from the end.

FOUR

GENERATING MATERIAL FOR SHORT SHORT STORIES

You will probably be surprised by what I tell you next. I want you to forget everything you've read about short short stories. I want you to start from scratch. The only stories that concern you here are your own, the ones you have yet to write. This applies to experienced writers as well as to those just beginning. In truth, you already know how to write short short stories. You knew how to write them before you ever heard of the form. As you will discover for yourself, this is not a "mystical" statement, nor is there a "trick" involved. What I present here instead are guidelines to follow so that nothing stands in your way.

THE SECRET TO WRITING SHORT SHORT STORIES

The method I'm about to present is not the *only* way to write short shorts, but I've seen it work over and over. Why? Because short short stories are associative, the result of what poet Robert Bly has called "leaping around the unconscious." The process of association is one in which random sensations, ideas, and memories become linked in our minds. These connections may be alien to our rational everyday ways of thinking, but they tend to have a logic all their own.

Psychoanalyst Carl Jung wrote that the unconscious is the store-house not only of our personal histories, but of our collective history as well. Jung's term "archetypes" refers to the memories, dreams, and images we share with others through the ages. So at the very least, your unconscious holds everything you've ever seen, felt, and imagined. If your unconscious were to hold no more than this, you would have enough material to write for a lifetime. So material is not the issue. What you have not been aware of is the way to *access* that material. But as you will soon find out, accessing the unconscious doesn't take any special skill. It does, however, involve *paying attention*. The secret of writing short short stories is paying attention to the unconscious and to its particular logic.

In this process, you are a receiver, a conduit for images, words, and sensations flowing freely through your consciousness. As you record them, you may feel as though your stories are writing themselves, as though you are only guiding the pen. Images, words, and sensations may rush forth like a waterfall. Or they may flow in a thin steady stream. At times, that flow may be no more than a trickle. The writer's job is not to tamper with the flow but to preserve it on paper before it ceases. The French poet Charles-Pierre Baudelaire referred to a similar process in the nineteenth century when he spoke of *attending to the prickings of consciousness*. But Kafka said it best.

> You do not need to leave your room. Remain sitting at your table and listen. Do not even listen, simply wait. Do not even wait, be quite still and solitary. The world will freely offer itself to you to be unmasked, it has no choice, it will roll in ecstasy at your feet.

GETTING READY TO WRITE

Before you do the exercises, you need to give up all your notions about writing well. Yes, I know you want to be a good writer, or you may already be one. That's fine. But your desires, aspirations, and judgments about writing well have nothing to do with the exercises. In fact, the last thing you want to do in the beginning is judge your work. This doesn't mean that judgment plays no part in the process. It does, but not in the beginning and not in the usual sense. What you will be judging is *energy* rather than *quality*, and you will only do that *after* you've finished writing.

Decide beforehand that whatever you put on the page will be okay. Give yourself freedom. Allow yourself to write whatever comes up. Some of the thoughts going through your mind may seem silly or nonsensical. Include them anyway. Let go of the critic before you start. You have no way of knowing what these initial exercises may lead to in the future. Even if you end up throwing out your exercise, your effort is not wasted. Nothing is wasted. Every effort is part of a larger process. I've found over and over that people bring certain preoccupations or obsessions to their writing. It's as though each one of us is *trying to get something right.* A writer may spend her entire lifetime trying. So don't be upset if you don't get it right the first time. If the ideas or images or sensations are important enough, they will keep coming back in your exercises; they will keep trying to work themselves out. There is a greater mind at work within us than the puny one that tells us we are wasting our time. The greater mind may be compared to an iceberg, extending way down below the surface. What we see is only the tip.

Before you sit down and do exercises, you need to let go of everything that stands between you and your writing. There's nothing wrong with dreaming your stories or novels will sell, but when you come to your desk to write exercises, make sure your dreams are as far from your mind as beans in Brazil. At other times, you may dream of impressing your family, your friends, your enemies, your acquaintances, people you don't even know, but while you engage in the process of writing, you need to leave all that behind. Forget your favorite authors, too. Role models won't help you here.

And forget yourself. If you listen to the chatter in your mind, you are not fully engaged in the writing. If you have a goal, such as writing well, for example, you will interfere with the process by *trying* too hard. The last thing you want to do is *try.* Instead, let things happen. Don't impose your will. *Don't take charge.*

Imagine yourself watching television. The screen, however, is *inside* your head and the program is playing only for you. But even you can't predict what you'll be seeing and hearing next on your screen. Those of you who are aural rather than visual—and this is important to know because it is part of your writing process—may imagine, instead of a television, a radio inside your head playing a program just for you.

As I said in the introductory chapter, writing is energy. The more you generate in a piece of writing, the more alive that writing will feel. Without energy, writing is dead. It's just words. So what is most important in this process is allowing the energy to flow. To do this, you must step out of your own way and let your unconscious take over. If you are worried or anxious or tense or thinking about your breakup with your boyfriend, chores that need to be done, or telephone calls that must be made, you will not be taking full advantage of this method.

Before you start, you need to clear your mind. Allow yourself time (even if it is only a few moments) to take some deep breaths. Be aware of the chatter running through your mind, but don't try to stop it; just be aware of it, and allow it to be there. Maybe you would like to turn down the volume. Try that. Imagine the voice or voices far away. Stand up and stretch or walk around the room. Separate the act of writing from other activities. If you approach your writing as though it is just another task, you will not be in the right frame of mind. You need to bring all of yourself to your writing. So whenever you sit down to write, preferably in a place that is both private and quiet, make sure you are ready to devote that time to nothing else, even if it is only for a few minutes.

The Five-Minute Exercise

Why five minutes? you may ask. Well, it's simple. If you have only five minutes to write, you won't have time to do anything else. You won't have time to worry, dream, or wonder about things. If you are to get your entire story on paper, which is the main objective of the exercise, you need to write quickly and spontaneously, without censoring your feelings or thoughts.

If the exercises were longer, you would have time to let your thoughts stop you. You might hear yourself say, "My mother would die if she ever read this!" or "My husband would leave me if he knew what I was writing." Or you might say, "This is really bad. I should probably take up weaving." Fortunately, in five minutes, you won't have much time for reflection.

Think of these exercises as training. You are not expected to record every detail. You can always "fill in" stories later when you revise. What you are going for initially is the plan or design, the "shape" of the piece. Knowing you have five minutes keeps you and the story moving. You can't get hung up describing one detail when you need to go from beginning to end within the time limit.

The exercises not only force you to write quickly and spontaneously, they force you to find your own voice. As I mentioned earlier, your voice is the one you hear inside your head. It is through your voice that readers get to know your deepest feelings and thoughts. Your voice reflects the particular way you see the world: your perceptions, emotions, and insights. No one sees the world in quite the way you do. Your voice may sound different at times, but it always sounds like you.

Some of you may still think of writing as an activity that is separate from the mind and body of the writer. If you had the chance, you might use a voice that sounds the way you think a writer *should* sound. When we try to impress others as being "smart" or "educated," for example, invariably we sound phony and strained. In five-minute exercises, however, you don't have time to *disguise* your voice.

Your voice will come through in spite of the roughness of your exercises. You will hear it in the rhythm, the choice of words, phrases, and expressions. Through listening to your voice repeatedly, you will learn to recognize it and become aware of times when it is out of sync, when it doesn't conform with your patterns of rhythm and speech.

The exercises serve one more basic purpose: They allow the unexpected to happen. By using this method, you will find yourself writing stories you never imagined. The excitement in using this method is that you never know in advance what you're going to write. See yourself as an explorer. You are about to enter unknown territory. When you tap the unconscious, you tap an infinite well. You need to be courageous enough to go places in yourself you've never been before. You need to be willing to look into your darkness as well as your light. You need to accept what you find there.

Plunging In

Let's say you've found a quiet and private place in which to write your exercises. You have a timer or stopwatch handy. You know everything you need to know to write: A story is a container for change; in a story, "something happens." But you have no idea *what* will happen in the one you will write. This uncertainty may make you a little anxious or a little excited, depending on who you are. That anxiety or excitement is energy. Use that energy as fuel.

Before you do the first one, I'd like to review exactly what you'll be doing. You're going to turn to the first page of exercises in section two of this book. Before you look at the exercises, however, set the timer for five minutes. Then look quickly over the list and pick one. Any exercise at all will be fine. Let's say you choose "Write a story about a lie."

Start writing the moment you choose the exercise. Many of you will be tempted to sit for a minute or so and figure out what to write. To avoid this as well as other temptations, it may be helpful, especially in the beginning, to do the exercises with a friend or two so you'll be less likely to cheat. Cheating makes little sense, of course, since in the end you'll only be cheating yourself.

You'll start with the first idea that comes to mind when you think about *a lie*. Many of you will find yourselves writing before you know what you are about to say. That's the best way to start. At the same time, you may experience a certain degree of discomfort, especially if this process is new to you. That's fine. Just keep going. You may be tempted to stop in the middle of the five minutes and read what you've written. If you find yourself doing this, let yourself go back to writing. Don't let your pen stop until the time is up. During this time, you will be in a zone that is much like free-falling. You will have no boundaries. These few minutes can be fun, even exhilarating, if you allow them to be.

As you write, you may be aware of the constant chatter in your mind. Don't let it interfere with your exercises. Acknowledge its presence and keep going. Don't try to stop it. If you use your energy to resist, you will be using energy better spent in your writing.

You may find yourself bombarded by images and sensations. They may come at you so fast you can't write quickly enough to get them all down. Do the best you can. Don't worry about spelling, punctuation, and grammar. Don't stop to correct dangling modifiers and incomplete sentences. If you stop to put in all the commas and colons and periods, you may interrupt the flow of words, which is far more important. Later, you will have plenty of time to make corrections. Right now you want to ride this wave of energy. You don't want to slow yourself down.

As you write, strong emotions may surface. They may feel unpleasant, or at the very least, uncomfortable. Allow them to be there. They have surfaced for a reason: There's something you need to deal with in your life, something you need to recognize. Strong emotions have tremendous energy attached to them. They may have been buried inside you for a long time. Don't resist them. Resisting is a way of trying to take control, which will stop the writing process.

If you let it, the anger or fear or sadness or disappointment you feel may disappear or transform itself as you write. Allow emotions to move through you. They are fluid. You may, in fact, experience a whole range of emotions while you write. They will not necessarily be painful ones. You may experience joy. You may experience spiritual or religious feelings. The deeper you go in your unconscious, the more you will find. At the end of five minutes, you may find a catharsis has taken place. You may feel freer, more alive than you've felt in years.

For some, the first exercise can be very different. You may find yourself feeling too little instead of too much. Words are streaming onto the paper, but that's the problem. The words are just words. They may be telling a story, but that story holds no charge, no energy. It's not *wrong* when this happens. It will probably happen to all of you at one time or another. Some exercises will leave you cold. Others will excite you. The same one that leaves you cold today may excite you next week.

When your exercise lacks energy, you may be drilling for oil in the wrong field so to speak, or you may be distancing yourself from feelings that are disturbing or painful or frightening. As a writer, however, you owe it to yourself to tell the truth. Writing is a process of self-exposure, a process of telling what you know so others can share in your "humanness." It is not enough to tell half-truths. If you are to create an experience in the reader, you must first create that experience in yourself.

Often, students tell me they find certain parts of their exercises "corny." Inevitably, the parts they find "corny" are the emotional ones readers enjoy most because they have felt similar emotions in similar circumstances. Your perspective may be unique, but what you feel is not. Whatever you feel, someone else has felt before you. But how you reveal those feelings and in what context is your own. If, instead, you suppress your emotions, you may not stop the flow of words, but you will rob your writing of energy. The words will not feel authentic. You will not feel deeply the roots of those words.

Your story should ring true. If it doesn't ring true to you, it won't ring true to others. The truth, however, is not dependent upon whether it actually happened. Sticking to the facts may limit your exercises and keep you from seeing what you need to tell. When exercises are read aloud in my classes and we discuss possible ways of revising them, I've heard many a student say in response to a suggestion, "But it didn't happen that way." Allow yourself to use the facts as springboards and leap from them. Facts don't change. But our interpretations of them do. What is "true" for you now may not have been true a year ago, a month ago, or even last week. Your exercises must reflect *your* truths. To do so, you may need to distort the facts or do away with them completely.

In stories, the truth is what feels true. The truth has nothing to do with facts. Events you record may have happened in reality, but it's not important for the reader to know that. When stories ring true, we *feel* those stories, sometimes deeply. For the writer and the reader, stories happen in the mind. When you are writing, you must give yourself the freedom to make up the truth. In my own stories, I follow this little motto:

> First it happens, then I make it up.

There is a wonderful little essay called "Figon, Georges," by the French writer Marguerite Duras. In it, she tells about a man who spent most of his life in prison. Duras relates that when the man was released, he wanted to write a book so he could tell everyone what prison life was like.

> Probably part of the trouble was . . . his desire to reproduce faithfully what had happened. He got . . . lost in the swamp of fact. If he'd forgotten everything and then reinvented it . . . he might not have died in despair. He ought to have cheated, recast for others what he had undergone himself.

This is what you need to do when you write about past events. There is no energy in *reproducing* life. Stories are not imitations of reality. They create new realities. The difference between creating and reproducing is the difference between painting a tree with broad brushstrokes and tracing its outline from a photo.

When an exercise triggers a memory, you need to recreate that memory as if it is happening now (even if the event happened long ago). The same holds true for what you are writing. You may relate something "true" about your past without using autobiographical data.

For example, writer Joel Agee represented a state of spiritual transformation he experienced in the 1960s by using the image of a "blue man." He was never *literally* a "blue man." The "blue man" is an invention, an image that came from his unconscious. Nevertheless, this image feels true.

You may start out fine, but halfway through the first exercise, your mind may go blank, the flow of words suddenly dries up. This is not a catastrophe. This is probably the result of fear. You may find yourself afraid of offending someone: a parent or lover perhaps, or an imaginary reader. You may be afraid of revealing yourself, afraid of showing others how you really feel. Writing may arouse a feeling similar to that of pulling down your pants in public. The point to remember is this: The public is not going to read your exercises. In fact, no one besides you is going to see them unless you decide to show them to someone else. When you revise your stories later, you may disguise characters and events, but before you can think of revision, you must get your stories on paper. Tell yourself before you start that the exercises are just for you. If, while writing, your discomfort continues, don't despair. This discomfort has great energy—you'll be able to break through your inhibitions and move on.

At the beginning, you won't be able to gauge exactly how long five minutes will be. It may seem too short, as though you have just gotten started. You'll need to work faster. As you do more exercises and become more accustomed to the process, however, you may find your stories fit more comfortably within the time slot. I've seen this happen again and again.

To others, five minutes may seem like an eternity. In fact, you may finish long before the five minutes are up. Whenever you reach what feels like the end of your exercise, stop. Don't try to continue. Wendy, one of my students, was upset and complained to me that she was unable to write for five minutes straight. By that time she had done ten or more exercises, so this feeling seemed to suggest a pattern. But when I read her exercises, I told her not to worry. She had written complete stories. Writing very short pieces was part of her process. If after finishing at least ten exercises, you find this is true for you as well, time them to three minutes instead. You may also do two exercises to write one story. Just set your timer. Choose an exercise and write. But don't try to finish. When you reach the end of three minutes, reset the timer, choose another exercise, and continue the story you started to its end, using the second topic as your theme.

Those of you who write longer than the five-minute limit may also claim that it's part of your writing process to need more than five minutes. If that's true, try setting your timer for seven or eight minutes and see what happens. If you find the time is still too short, go back to writing for five minutes. The problem may be that you are afraid to plunge into an exercise. Instead, you write a prologue or preface. You are marking time until you have the courage to really begin. You are jumping up and down on the diving board instead of going straight into the water. While you are marking time, you are searching for the story instead of letting the story find you. You need to plunge in as soon as your timer goes off.

The Time Is Up

Let's say you've done an exercise and now the time is up. You read what you've written. The first question to ask yourself is whether you've been able to get the entire story on paper. If not, you might want to give yourself an extra minute to finish. While you want to abide by the five-minute rule, you don't want to be so rigid that you don't allow yourself to finish a story that you know needs only a few more lines. You want to enjoy this process.

Okay, let's say you're really finished. You reread what you've written. Now ask yourself if the story surprises you. Have you written something you didn't expect to write? Even if you've written about a familiar incident or event in your life, have you seen it from a new angle? Have you discovered something you didn't realize before? If so, you're on the right track.

The Energy Scale

Now is the time for evaluating, but as I've said before, the evaluation has nothing to do with judging the writing as good or bad. What is important here is judging whether your exercise has energy. An exercise that excites or interests you has energy. One that bores you does not.

To evaluate the energy in your exercise or first draft, note on a scale of one to ten your level of interest or excitement. In other words, you will be judging each first draft by the way it makes you feel, not by the quality of the writing. You will have plenty of time later to fool around with the words and revise them. What you are looking for now is a feeling of excitement. If what you have written holds no energy for you, if it rates a one on the scale, simply throw it away. It is highly unlikely that you will breathe life into a piece of dead writing. And why would you want to? If there's no energy in the exercise, your heart wasn't in it anyway. And if it was dead for you, believe me when I say that it will be dead for others, too. There are many exercises. Some of them will not excite you. Find the ones that do.

On the following pages you'll find three first drafts written by students. Each rated her exercise high on the energy scale. All of these exercises have vitality. As I said, this energy is what you'll be looking for in your own exercises. You may also look to see if your exercises are complete like those of Nomi, Amanda, and Carol. This means the stories go from beginning to end within the time limit and either reach surprising conclusions or offer unexpected perspectives.

For the sake of readability, I have decided against using reproductions of the original handwritten drafts. In one or two instances, I have made minor corrections in the text, also for the sake of readability. The exercises presented here are cleaned-up versions, but they are still the students' words.

The way to approach these exercises is to look at them as possibilities, not as finished stories, though in each of these three, the plan or design of each piece is already in place.

Nomi Altabef wrote this exercise at The New School in response to a photographic image of an old man and an old woman sitting on a park bench.

MEETING

It's been a while since I thought of anyone but my Franny. She's been gone twenty years and although I missed her, cried even, I just kept up with the business and now, after exactly twenty years since she's been gone, I am here, on our park bench for the first time. The woman sitting next to me has her hair, her legs, her lean toward the sea, and when she turns her face toward me I will know, after twenty years, if she has come to open my heart again, or if it is my time to go.

Amanda Gardner wrote this first draft in my private workshop in response to the exercise "Write a story about greed."

GREED

Greedy. Greedy. Greedy. She tried not to be. She tried to want less but she inevitably asked for more than her share. I mean, my God, how could she justify breathing so much air when there were people suffering from asthma and dying of cystic fibrosis? And here she was able to take in huge gulps of pure air any time she wanted. Oops, did I inhale too deeply? She tried taking shorter breaths but it made her head spin and she was afraid she wouldn't concentrate enough on what people were saying and they wouldn't feel interesting. She tried to pause for long times between breaths but that made her gasp and she was afraid she was being too loud. She tried alternating between her mouth and her nose but figured that probably didn't make any difference anyway. She even thought about killing herself but then if she was cremated she'd be befouling the very air little children would need to breathe.

Carol Mager, also a student in one of my private workshops, wrote this story in response to the exercise "Write a story about a child."

STAND-OFF

The mother, dressed in a loose black coat, leather boots and turtleneck, bent slightly at the waist as she faced her son. The little boy, six or seven, his down jacket flapping with the breeze, dark red hair neatly combed, jumped up and down in frustration and rage. His yellow backpack, filled with the tools of school, moved in syncopated rhythm to his body. Tears left wet marks on his shirt as they rolled off his plump cheeks.

She tried to hear him, even as the wind ripped away the words between them. Her stern face was fixed with emotion, the stiffness of her body closing the door on any opportunity for compromise.

An elderly man, a stranger to them both, passed by, his little white dog straining on the leash, pulling the man along. Sensing him observing her, the mother looked up into his face. He smiled slightly and nodded his head, acknowledging her distress.

As if the white haired man had some magical powers, the child quieted suddenly, his attention diverted to the toy-like dog who was dancing around his legs, begging for a smile.

The struggle between mother and son evaporated like a sudden fog. Without another word, she took his hand and they continued on their way.

You may find that your exercises are not as complete as these three examples. The plan or design in your first drafts may need more work. In other words, your exercises may not have a definite "shape." If so, this is not cause for worry, as you will see in the next chapter on revision.

Before reading further, however, I suggest you do some exercises on your own. In fact, I want you to keep doing exercises until you feel comfortable working this way. For example, you may find the first one a breeze, but the second and third may be harder. Any number of scenarios are possible. Just keep going, whether the exercises feel easy or hard, whether you "like" doing them or not. Not every exercise will be fun, but enough of them should be enjoyable enough to keep you excited. If you're having a hard time, it probably means you are being critical; you're not allowing yourself to play. If this is the case, go back and reread this chapter. Writing exercises are a form of play. Allow yourself to have fun, and follow these last directions below.

If you can, set aside thirty minutes at a time to do a series of six exercises. Before you do, read the introduction in chapter six, which will show you various ways of choosing the exercises. Set the timer before choosing a single one. If you are choosing a series of exercises, the same rule applies. Even when you've chosen a series of six, however, you'll need to reset the timer every five minutes until you have finished all of them. It's not necessary to stop and read each exercise before going on to the next. Remember when you do read that you're only looking for energy. What you'll do with that energy is the subject of the following chapter.

FIVE

SHAPING AND POLISHING SHORT SHORT STORIES

Now that you've written a minimum of ten exercises, you are ready for the next part of the process, which is revision. To help clarify the process, I will use examples from my students' work.

WHAT IS REVISION?

Revision is the process of correcting or improving your exercises. It involves decision making that leads to the discovery of your story. You will use both intuition and logic to make decisions. I see this process as a kind of juggling act in which you go back and forth between logic and intuition, weighing each decision as you work. Often your choices will be wrong, especially in the beginning. What is most important, however, is allowing yourself to make wrong decisions and to learn from your mistakes.

Some say revision is ninety percent of writing. I don't know if I agree, but I will say that few writers feel their first drafts are perfect. You may, however, be one of those who writes a perfect or nearly perfect short short. It does happen, but most of you will find your initial efforts need work.

When you do exercises for the first time, you run the risk of becoming unduly attached to your words. You may tend to regard them as "sacred." You're afraid to make changes, afraid you'll *ruin* what you wrote. It's true some first drafts emerge from the unconscious with such ease they seem magical or mystical, but this feeling is no guarantee you've been graced by the gods. I have emphasized the importance of feeling. The more you write, the more you will be able to trust your feelings, your instincts. At the beginning, however, your instincts may be less than trustworthy. Often you will find upon re-reading your exercise (sometimes you'll need a few days to gain perspective) that your unconscious doesn't have the last word after all.

Building the Story

This first act of revision is merely an extension of the unconscious process you began using in the previous chapter. But here you are directing it toward the goal of finishing a particular story in a way that excites you.

Some exercises will be more complete than others; they will have a definite shape, that is, a design or plan, as in the first drafts of Nomi, Amanda, and Carol in the previous chapter. This section is for those of you who still need to work on the structure or shape of your exercises.

The first draft you choose to revise is one that has energy, one that excites and interests you more than the others, even if it does not yet have a clear shape or design. It will be helpful to ask yourself exactly what excites you. When you look closely, you may find that the exercise leaves you cold except for a single phrase or sentence like this one from Carol's piece.

> Her anger roasted the air between them as the car sped
> through the night.

If only a phrase or fragment or single sentence excites you, use it as the beginning of a new exercise. Time yourself for five minutes and write.

Perhaps several sentences grab you but the ending feels dead, or the exercise feels as though it takes a turn in the wrong direction. If this is the case, time yourself for two or three minutes and continue from the last sentence that excites you.

The idea is to create as much stimulating *raw material* in a single exercise as you can. The more you have to work with from the start, the less you will have to revise. You may find yourself discarding two or three exercises before coming up with one that has a shape or design that stirs you. Later, you will find it easier to eliminate words rather than add them to your story, so don't be afraid of writing too much, though you don't want to go over the time limit.

Uncovering the Story

In this case, you've written *more* than you need. The exercise you have chosen may have an overall shape or plan, but its point or meaning may not be clear. If so, revision will be a process of *uncovering* the story. In other words, you may have to *separate* the story from your exercise. When you look at what you've written, it may be helpful to ask yourself these questions:

1. What happens in this exercise?
2. Where is the change?
3. What is the main thrust or focus?

Once you've answered these, the parts of your exercise that digress or seem irrelevant may be eliminated. Often, beautiful sentences will have to be cut because they don't advance the story. (I'll talk more about this soon.)

This process of uncovering the story makes me think of the sculptor who sees the portrait in the stone before he carves it. He may not have a complete picture in his mind. In fact, it may be fuzzy at best, but he knows enough to start chipping away. Once you *see or have a feeling for* the basic story in your exercise, like the sculptor you can chip away at words that feel unnecessary.

HOW TO KNOW IF YOUR STORY NEEDS REVISION

Let's say you're sure your exercise has energy and you're reasonably certain there is a shape to it. Where do you go from here?

How about listening to your exercise? What does it sound like when you read it out loud? Listening to yourself on a tape recorder is preferable because it will give you a degree of objectivity, unlike listening to yourself read aloud. What you should be aware of is whether you are stumbling while you read. If so, take note of the places where you stumble. Each of you has an inner rhythm. It is evident in the way you walk, in your breathing, in your patterns of speech. It is part of you. There is also a rhythm in the words you write. When that rhythm is off, you tend to stumble in your speech. The words that cause you to stumble probably have either too many or too few syllables to fit the particular rhythm of a phrase or sentence. You may also be stumbling because the words don't feel right for other reasons. Faulty rhythm may be symptomatic of other problems. Perhaps the words are not specific enough or their meanings are wrong or unclear. Perhaps for the sake of brevity, you have left out details important for the reader to know, or it may be that certain words are out of tone. This means they stand out from the others. They may sound "phony." They may be words you don't ordinarily use. Wherever you stumble, you can be sure there's a reason. Look for it. Find other words that *feel* better.

If you are "fuzzy" about the meaning or proper usage of any word in your exercise, look it up in the dictionary. Get into the habit of using a dictionary, a thesaurus, and a guide such as *The Elements of Style*, by William Strunk and E.B. White. You can't write well without grasping the essentials of grammar. If you don't want to spend your time referring to or studying these resources, perhaps writing is not for you. You would not construct a house without having all the tools you need and the knowledge to use them. The same holds true for language. There are no shortcuts to using language correctly. In a very short story, every word counts.

As you read your story, visualize it. Try to *see* every image in your mind. Are the images clear? Karen's story begins like this.

> Mama was as cruel as ever. In her starched white apron, she appeared at our door and brought the traditional newlywed cake, but she failed to fill it with charms that would bring us good fortune. Instead, I found a button that belonged to a smock my dead sister had worn. I cried when I saw what it was. Mama smiled.

It's easy for us to visualize the sadistic mother, in her "starched white apron," smiling, as her daughter finds in the cake the button belonging to her dead sister.

Reread your story. If you can't *see* every image you have written, your descriptions probably need work. Whether you are describing *physical events* (such as the ones in Karen's story) or *inner states*, your words need to be clear and precise. Consider the opening of Robert's story "The Lie."

> He told her that he loved her but it was a lie. He knew as the words fell from his mouth that he was locking himself in his own prison, but he was pulled along like a stone rolling down a hill.

Here Robert vividly portrays a paradoxical state of mind resulting from a physical event, in this case, the telling of a lie. The narrator describes a man who feels both trapped ("he was locking himself in his own prison") and out of control ("he was pulled along like a stone rolling down a hill"). I think, in this instance, the two contradictory images clearly portray the character's conflict.

After reading your exercise aloud and checking the definition and usage of words you are unsure about, you may still not know what—if anything—needs improvement. Some of you may be aware of places in your story that feel weak, but you may not know exactly what is wrong. Or maybe you can identify the problem, but you don't know how to solve it. If either of these scenarios sounds familiar, I suggest you put the exercise aside for at least several days, and choose the next one to revise. Go as far as you can without difficulty. When you come to a place where you don't know what to do, stop. Don't bang your head against the wall. There is only so much a writer can see at a single sitting. Time will give you new perspective on your work.

If, however, you hate to stop writing even when you know you're stuck, there are certain tricks that may help you. Instead of stopping your work completely, allow yourself to take frequent breaks. Sometimes, making coffee or phoning a friend is all you need. Directing your attention away from the exercise, even for a few minutes, takes the pressure off and may give you more perspective when you return. It may also free your unconscious enough to find solutions you couldn't work out through reason alone.

This next trick is more extreme, but it may work for those of you who become very frustrated or upset when you can't make an exercise work the way you want and you've run out of things to try. In the moment you give up on your exercise, which means you stop fighting to get it right, you create space for the unconscious to do its work. Again, you take the pressure off yourself. This act of giving up, however, needs to be sincere. It's a process of yielding to the momentary despair or frustration that writing sometimes brings. It doesn't mean you have to give up on the story forever, but you must feel that way in the moment in order for this to work.

To summarize, pay attention to how you feel about what you have written. Is something in the exercise bothering you? Be aware of those places that don't feel right. You may not trust your feelings at this point, but you have to start somewhere so it is best to give yourself the benefit of the doubt. Change what you think needs changing. If your edits don't work, try again, or put the exercise away for a while. The more decisions you make, the better. The results of those decisions are less important right now. I suggest you save all the changes you make, *even those that don't work*. You will find them useful if you need to retrace your steps, especially if you go in the wrong direction and lose the energy in your piece. You may also use the questions below as guidelines to help you revise.

QUESTIONS TO ASK YOURSELF WHILE REVISING

These questions are intended to train you to look at your story from different angles. You may find that some questions overlap or seem to say the same thing. If you were carving a sculpture, you would want to see it from every side. The same holds true with stories. There are different ways of seeing the same short short.

Does Your Short Short Feel True?

A story that feels true expresses the writer's intuitions of reality and causes the reader to have an experience. There may be no words other than the writer's words that can cause this particular experience to happen in the reader.

Meaning comes from feeling. A short short that feels true makes you think, *Yes! That's the way life is.* The story seems as though it really happened (whether it did or not is irrelevant). Or the story feels as though it *might* have happened; in other words, what takes place *feels* possible. Or the short short may be so engaging that the reader willingly suspends disbelief in order to enter a world that is obviously impossible. This happens in surreal or fantastic short shorts that feel true. So a story that feels true moves the reader—and the writer! If you aren't moved by your own words, you can bet others will not be moved either.

Does the Short Short Make Sense?

Every short short has an internal logic. In Rebecca's, a father leaves his terrified daughter to cross a crowded street alone. The narrator describes her as she crosses.

Her feet are encased in concrete blocks.

As a reader, this sentence stopped me. I wondered if her feet were *literally* encased in concrete blocks. In a surrealistic story, this line might be fine. Strange things happen in surrealistic stories. But Rebecca's story seems otherwise naturalistic. If Rebecca wants me, the reader, to understand this image as a metaphor for the way the girl feels, rather than a literal statement of fact, she might, for example, make this statement.

Her feet feel as though they are encased in concrete blocks.

If, however, the girl's feet are literally encased in concrete blocks, this is something so unusual, so extreme and unexpected, that in order for the reader to accept this as true, Rebecca must tell how this happened and why.

For a story to make sense, every element must seem plausible *within the context* the writer has created. If the writer has created a context in which purple men kill orange men, the presence of pink tigers and green giraffes will make sense.

Does Every Sentence Carry the Story a Little Farther Toward Its Conclusion?

In short shorts, there are no wasted words. Every word should advance the story. If words are there for any other reason—such as, "Oh, what a beautiful sentence I've written!"—get rid of them. I hate to sound harsh, but there is no other way to say this. Beautiful sentences don't belong in a short short unless they impart information essential to the story. In general, the role of each sentence is to tell the reader at least a little bit more. This keeps the story moving.

A story that may seem to contradict this is Robert Walser's "Nothing At All" (see chapter two), in which the author repeats the same words over and over. But this repetition reflects the wife's thoughts going in circles; her inability to make a decision is the point of the story.

Does the Story Have a Logical Sequence of Events?

Barbara, who is otherwise intelligent and accomplished, was being careless when she failed to notice the following problems in her exercise.

> A man finds his bedroom closet empty. He opens it. "I sold them!" yells his wife in the kitchen when the man says, "Where are all my clothes?"

Obviously, the man must open the closet door before he can see that the closet is empty. The next sentence, which begins with an answer rather than a question, is not wrong, but it is an awkward construction. It makes more sense for the man to ask where his clothes are before the wife tells him. This is how Barbara revised these sentences.

> A man opens his bedroom closet and finds it empty. "Where are all my clothes?" he yells to his wife in the kitchen. "I sold them!" she says.

Are You Giving Enough Information? Too Much Information?

This is a crucial question in a short short. How much should you say? Writing a short short is a little bit like walking on a tightrope. It's easy to go over the line, easy to take a wrong turn. Knowing what to leave in and what to take out comes with practice, experience, and trust in your instincts.

In the meantime, look for the spine of your story: What feels most important in your exercise? Look for loose ends: characters, details, actions, or events left unresolved. For example, have you introduced a character who disappears after being mentioned only once? If so, is that character necessary? Everything in a short short needs to be related, no matter how disparate the characters, objects, or actions seem to be.

For example, in Robert Kelly's short short "Rosary," there is a deer, which the protagonist sees while walking in the country. This seems relatively unimportant until the poet returns to the deer at the end and relates it to the woman in the story who may have seen "the same deer."

> Or not the same: who can tell one animal from another?

In this short short, which describes two people alone at night who never actually meet, he uses the image of the deer to connect them and wrap up the story.

In this next short short, Amanda Gardner gives the reader the bare bones of a story, but in this case, that is enough.

THE TEA PARTY

There are teacups and a lace cloth on the table. The table is cheap but the cloth and cups are fine quality. She fit the cloth and the cups in the bag she took with her when she crawled on her belly through mud-slimed grass to freedom.

Her new wage could buy cheap clothes in a neighborhood known for its poor immigrants but it could never buy fine bone china and lace. It could never buy a connection with the past.

Every week on her day off she buys pastries from the Hungarian bakery on 82nd Street. She takes out the teacups and the lace cloth. She makes tea in an aluminum kettle and she visits with her three good friends, all of whom were killed in the escape.

There are few details, but each one tells the reader something important. Instead of stating directly that the woman escaped from Hungary, Amanda is more subtle: ". . . on her day off she buys pastries from the Hungarian bakery. . . ." Besides the fact that she escaped with her lace and china, we know nothing about her, and yet we, as readers, can understand the loneliness of an immigrant woman in a strange country, missing the friends from her past. The story could have happened in any number of places and represents to my mind a universal condition.

Amanda's style is sparse. She uses few adjectives, for instance. Not all short shorts are sparse, but they are economical when it comes to using language. In the hands of another writer, Amanda's theme might be far more emotional, for instance. How much you, the writer, choose to say is a personal decision that depends on your style and sensibility.

Are You Using Many Words to Describe Something That Can Be Said With Just a Few?

Notice how in Chekhov's short short "The Nincompoop" (presented in chapter two), essential information about the governess's past is revealed by a single line of dialogue.

"In other places I was not given all . . ."

This sentence tells the reader that the governess has allowed previous employers to cheat her. It reveals her character and makes her present behavior understandable. The reader doesn't need to know any other facts about the woman's previous employers. This is the only fact that is relevant to the story.

Or consider the example below from John's exercise. In it, a couple argue. The wife is screaming at her husband for gambling away money that could have paid for repairs on their rundown home. Since the focus of the story is the argument rather than the house, the house is secondary. In revising this story, John found that he could render the appearance of the house by using a few striking images instead of the detailed description of its flaws that occupied far more space than the argument in his first draft. Here is part of his detailed description.

> The roof leaked. Three of the steps leading up to the house were broken. The rail on the porch was broken. Inside, the floorboards were rotting, the paint was peeling, the toilet was stopped up.

He reduced this to one sentence.

> The roof leaked, the floorboards were rotting, paint peeled off the walls.

When he further revised the story, he found that he didn't need to describe the house at all. He could reveal its major flaws in dialogue.

> "With that money, we could have fixed that leaking roof and replaced the rotting floorboards. We could have painted these peeling walls!" the wife screamed.

Will the Reader Be Able to Reach Your Conclusion and Believe It?

The ending of a short short must feel intrinsic to the whole. It should never feel tacked on. Your unconscious is usually better at finding the ending than your rational mind. If the conclusion doesn't come easily, put it aside for a while. If you reread the exercise later in a relaxed state, the ending may come instantly. If it doesn't, continue for a minute or two, starting from the point where it loses energy or goes in the wrong direction.

In Susan Bassik's short short titled "The Decision to Part," the reader doesn't know at the beginning why the narrator is anxious when she tells the man in the story she doesn't think she should see him, but his violent behavior makes it clear by the end why the narrator would want to break off this relationship and why she would feel unable to do so.

THE DECISION TO PART

"I don't think I should see you any more." The quivering voice belonged to me. It lacked conviction but I breathed a sigh of relief once the words were out.

He looked at me pensively and was silent. Mistaking his silence for agreement, I rushed on. "That doesn't mean we can't still be friends, you know, go out for coffee sometimes or maybe even the movies. We always like the same movies, don't we? Or, I know, we can meet once a month, maybe on the first day, or maybe on the last day. Something like that. Do you think that's a good idea?"

He reached out swiftly and grabbed my wrist, twisting my arm as he pulled me towards him. "No, I don't think so," he said. His voice was as hard as his grip and it was then that I realized the decision to part would have to be his.

COMMON PROBLEMS

Some of the problems presented here may seem basic to you. Frequently, they result from carelessness. The problems I am referring to specifically include not enough detail; abstraction; unclear, incorrect, or ineffective word choices; overloading sentences; telling rather than showing; weak dialogue; and changes in tone. I also include here problems with beginnings and endings.

Most of these problems are not unique to short shorts. They occur in longer fiction as well, but the way these problems occur and their solutions are often unique to the short short form. The examples, like the previous ones in this chapter, are from the stories of my students. The solutions presented are not the only solutions possible. There are no absolutes when it comes to writing short shorts (or any other kind of fiction for that matter).

Every story is different. What works in one may not work in another. Nevertheless, the more familiar you become with these problems, the faster you will recognize them in your own work. I encourage you to look for more than one way to solve whatever problems you may find in your own stories.

If revising fiction is new for you, it may take some time to adjust to the process. After the spontaneity of doing exercises, you may feel uncomfortable making conscious decisions. This discomfort may translate itself into a stiff style of writing or, at the very least, a style that feels less natural. Remember, your voice feels comfortable. It takes no special effort to write. If your voice feels forced, try saying out loud what you are trying to write. That should help you stay with your voice. When you *try* to imitate others or *try* to sound the way you *think* you should, you are likely to get yourself in trouble.

My next statement is more important than anything else I say in this chapter. *If you feel yourself losing the initial excitement while reworking a story, stop! You're going in the wrong direction.* Whatever revisions you make—whether they result from intuition or logic—must *feel* right in the moment you are making them even if you change your mind later on. If the piece begins to feel dead, backtrack to the point where it lost energy and start the process of revising again.

Slow Openings

You may discover that your first paragraph presents information that is irrelevant to your story. Sometimes the first paragraph is more like a warm-up than a beginning. You may find that the story really begins in the second or third paragraph. This happens in Steven's short short, which presents an encounter between Jim, an American man, and Ase, a Swedish woman, on board a ship crossing the North Sea. Steven begins the short short like this.

> Jim stood at the rail as his MGB was hoisted on board at Newcastle for the North Sea crossing to Sweden. He admired its classic lines with pride, like a proud parent watching a toddler in a playground. His solo motor tour of England, Wales and Scotland had been adventurous.

Jim's car is not mentioned again and neither is his motor tour. Steven said he chose this beginning to give the reader a sense of who Jim is. But since the story is about an encounter between Jim and Ase, unless the car and motor tour have something to do with what transpires between them, both are unnecessary. The reader needs to learn who

Jim is *in relation* to Ase. Steven does not introduce her, however, until the third paragraph when he is a quarter of the way through the story.

> Ase, a Swedish woman, in a bulky cardigan and horn-rimmed glasses, sidled up to him at the bar.

When Steven revised this story, he began this way.

> Jim, an American, was standing at the bar on board a ship crossing the North Sea from Newcastle to Sweden, when Ase, a Swedish woman, in a bulky cardigan and horn-rimmed glasses, sidled up to him.

This first line focuses his short short.

The reader needs a *hook* that will draw her into a story. That hook is an event, a character, an action, or an image the reader can clearly imagine. Take this opening line, for instance, in "Tonight Is a Favor to Holly," a slightly longer story, by the minimalist Amy Hempel.

> A blind date is coming to pick me up, and unless my hair grows an inch by seven o'clock, I am not going to answer the door.

This sentence has specific details: the blind date, the hair, the decision not to answer the door. These are details a reader can imagine. They reveal the character. Reading a story without a hook is like trying to climb the side of a mountain without footholds. There's nothing to hang on to, or, at the very least, not enough.

You want the opening of your story to intrigue, interest, or excite both you and the reader. Imagine the short short as a mountain and the footholds as physical details. If there are not enough physical details, or if those details are abstract rather than concrete—which means they may be too theoretical or impersonal—the reader will have difficulty following your short short. Physical details are the building blocks of a story. They lure the reader *inside* the story; the words become pictures or sense objects in the reader's mind. The following sentence about Ase lacks concrete details in Steven's story.

> She talked about the need to live free of the expectations of her family.

What are her family's expectations? His sentence is too vague, too general. It doesn't tell us enough about Ase. Here's the revision.

She said her family expected her to be married and respectable, but she wanted to be free.

These details are more specific. They give the reader a sense of who Ase is. By saying "she wanted to be free," he paves the way for their spending the night in her cabin. He could have been even more specific, however. He could have defined exactly what freedom means for her. For example, he could have said she believed in free love, but that would have said too much since we find out later that both parties tell different versions of what took place that night. The reader is not sure what happened. The word *free* in this case is specific enough. It leaves a bit to the reader's imagination. Once you see the thrust or focus in your own short short, ask yourself if every detail is necessary to make your point.

You want to be precise, but you don't want to dwell on minor details. This will slow down the story and blur its focus. For example, in order for the reader to imagine a woman drinking a glass of water, the writer need not describe every microscopic movement of her hand between the moment she picks up the glass to the moment she tastes the water. If you are new to writing short shorts, you may be inclined to write minute descriptions of actions or events better left unsaid or, at most, simply stated.

To describe a forest, you would emphasize the details about the forest that are most relevant to your story. The point of view will determine what you describe. If, for example, your narrator describes getting lost, you might emphasize how all the trees look alike.

If you get stuck trying to find the right word or phrase, you might ask yourself how you would say it if you were talking to a friend about the person, thing, event, or action you are describing on paper. Talk about it out loud, preferably into a tape recorder. Talking stops you from thinking about it. You may also find that the word or phrase giving you the most trouble is unnecessary. Check to see how the story sounds without that particular thought or idea.

Mechanical Errors

In the beginning, you may not be aware of clumsy writing, misused words, or incorrect grammar, but the more you write, and the more you read, the more you will become conscious of sentences that don't work, especially if you make it your business to study sentences that do. The following error in Margot's story is a common one.

> The smoke was pitch black. Robert and I crawl on hands
> and knees, coughing, our eyes burning.

Margot had to decide whether she wanted her story about a fire to happen in past or present tense. She decided on present tense because it gives the story—which is very dramatic—an immediacy lacking in the past tense.

> The smoke is pitch black. Robert and I crawl on hands and
> knees, coughing, our eyes burning.

It may be that you are trying to give too much information in a single sentence. In Rob's story, for instance, an old man is being secretly observed from the fire escape by the narrator.

> With a wry smile, he rises and snatches a pair of suspend-
> ered, khaki trousers from the foot of the bed and makes his
> way across the room to a make-shift kitchen that includes a
> sink, hot-plate and ironing board, which substitutes for a table
> and has on one end, a few plates, and a glass, where he begins
> pressing the wrinkles out of his trousers.

What is disturbing in this sentence is both the placement and wording of the clause "which substitutes for a table and has on one end, a few plates, and a glass." It stands between the ironing board and the act of the man pressing his trousers. The phrase takes the reader out of the story by breaking up the image the reader has formed in his mind of the man crossing the room to iron his pants. Rob revised this sentence.

> With a wry smile, he rises and snatches a pair of suspend-
> ered, khaki trousers from the foot of the bed and makes his
> way across the room to a make-shift kitchen that includes a
> sink, hot-plate, and an ironing board, used also as a table-top,
> where he begins pressing the wrinkles out of his trousers.

By eliminating the unnecessary clause, the reader is able to follow the old man's actions without interruption. The phrase "used also as a table-top" is included so that the function of the ironing board in the kitchen doesn't seem strange and stop the reader.

If you find yourself writing long or complicated sentences and you're not sure they work or are grammatically correct, consider keeping your sentences simple by using a single idea in each one until you have reviewed enough grammar and feel confident enough to handle longer constructions. At the same time, vary your sentences. You don't want each one to start with a pronoun or all of them to be the same length, for example. Boring writing is often born from these practices, but there are always exceptions. At the risk of being boring, when in doubt, use the simple word. Use language that feels natural, that comes easily.

Unclear Writing

When writing is unclear, it stops the reader. It's as though the reader were climbing a staircase and suddenly found a step missing. There is a gap, a lack of continuity in these sentences from Tina's story, which takes place on a farm.

> Trudy's made another omelet for dinner. It's the biggest drawback to all those chickens.

Reading this, I felt something was left out. What's the biggest drawback to all those chickens? I wondered. When I asked Tina, she said they lay too many eggs. She meant that making omelets was the best way to use up all the eggs laid by the chickens, but she didn't say that. This kind of error is more easily discovered when reading aloud to another person. You may be quite surprised to find discrepancies between what you think you have written and what someone else understands. Here are Tina's revised sentences.

> Trudy's made another omelet. It's the best way to use up all those eggs the chickens lay.

Clumsy writing may also be unclear. At the very least, it is awkwardly constructed. This line comes from Judy's story.

> The next day Daniel could not understand as Anne began to rage and accuse him of responding to her sister's flirting.

I understand what Judy means when she says ". . . as Anne began to rage and accuse him . . . ," but the verb *began* weakens the active verbs that follow. When she says, ". . . responding to her sister's flirting," I wasn't sure if *he* was flirting or not—it's too vague. Judy revised the sentence.

> The next day Daniel could not understand Anne's rage when she accused him of flirting with her sister.

The active verbs make the sentence stronger and clearer. They give the reader more to "see" in a story.

Shifting Point of View

The error I encounter most often with point of view is one in which a character knows far more than he should. In other words, the point of view is inconsistent. In David's story, a man frequents a Korean grocery, owned by Mr. and Mrs. Kim. He doesn't know these people very well, but he offers to help their fourteen-year-old daughter when he sees her having a problem with algebra. The story is told from the man's point of view. When he offers his help, the girl's mother responds like this.

> Mrs. Kim's face brightened. She was always on the look-out for a chance to further her daughter's education.

The narrator can *see* Mrs. Kim's face brighten, but how would he know that Mrs. Kim is always looking for a chance to further her daughter's education? He barely knows these people. His only contact with them is through their store. David changed this sentence to reflect the narrator's point of view.

> Mrs. Kim's face brightened. She struck me as the kind of woman who wouldn't turn down a chance to further her daughter's education.

Weak Dialogue

Your story may have a consistent viewpoint but suffer from weak dialogue. Dialogue must reveal the character of the speaker. You need to capture each character's particular way of speaking. If that means using bad grammar or sentence fragments, do so. If it means being "long-winded," however, you'd do best to make it concise and give the reader the *flavor* of the words without using lengthy sentences. Dialogue must reveal something that the reader needs to know. Decide if every line is necessary to advance your story.

You want to avoid speech patterns that sound awkward and stilted as in this example from Mark's short short.

> "Pray for the wind," I said to my wife. "I wish it to rush into my lungs once the plane doors open, and cleanse me for good of everything I once supposed, assumed, and insisted was true."

Can you picture this speaker? I can't. The words sound "full of air" to me. The phrase "supposed, assumed, and insisted" is too vague to reveal the character or advance the story and simply rings false.

To create dialogue that feels alive, you need to *be* that character. Like an actor, you need to get "inside the character's head." In these next lines from Sandra's short short, the conversation sounds natural. You hear real people speaking. Description in this case helps the reader visualize the characters.

> She lifted the small child onto the butcher block table and opened the yellow checked curtains in the middle of the afternoon so she could see out the kitchen window. "Look out there, child," she said, in a slow southern drawl.
> "What am I looking at Mama?"
> "The darkness, child. The darkness. There's gonna be a summer storm."

Telling Rather Than Showing

Instead of adding to the story, dialogue sometimes duplicates what has already been said through description. In other words, you may be *telling* and *showing* the same thing, as in this example from Gloria's story.

> Just then the real mother came over to thank me for finding her child.
> She said, "God is good and I hope many blessings come to you and your family. I can't thank you enough for what you did."

First the narrator says that the real mother thanked her. Then she tells the reader what she said when she thanked her. I would choose the real mother's voice over the flat description simply because it says more. It gives the reader a sense of the real mother's gratitude. It shows rather than tells.

Telling instead of showing is a common problem in short shorts. It's true that telling often takes less words, and when you are trying to pass quickly from one point to another and need a transition between two actions or events, telling is often cleaner and faster. But it doesn't give the reader the same experience. When you tell, the reader has to take your word for it.

If the action or event is important to the story, allow the reader to experience it by showing. For example, in her story, Diane could have said this about the "three women" sitting on "a low brick wall."

> They ate their lunches.

Instead, she chose to show them eating their lunches:

> They bit into their overstuffed sandwiches, each one wiping her mouth intermittently with a rough paper napkin.

Ineffective Tone

A story shows a certain attitude. That attitude may be described as the tone. A change of tone in a short short shifts the *manner* in which the story is being told. Such changes occur when there's a variation in style or mood. For example, you may say something is out of tone when dialogue is uncharacteristic of the speakers. The words you choose create the tone. In a short short, problems usually occur when the tone isn't consistent or, to say it another way, it is out of sync with the content.

A story may be told in a carefree, lighthearted manner, as is Carol's surrealistic story in which a woman dances with the devil and turns into one herself. In the process, the narrator finds her memories (of normal everyday life) fleeing faster than "Picasso's dove of peace." The phrase feels out of tone because the reference to Picasso seems too "high-minded" for this story. Also, a dove doesn't denote speed and it seems too gentle an image for a short short about becoming a devil.

Reading a short short that contains an out-of-tone phrase reminds me of looking at a row of beetle specimens in a glass case and suddenly coming upon a bee. My first thought is, *What's that doing here?*

Weak Endings

You may have managed to avoid most of the problems presented here, but it's possible you're still not happy with the ending of your story. If this is the case, go back and look at the beginning for an image that may tie the threads together. Your first paragraph may contain the ending. Early in Dalia's amusing short short about a girl starting a job in the produce department of a supermarket, Pablo, the manager, makes this remark.

"Nice to meet you Sally, you remind me of a tomato."

She says she "stayed quiet and questioned her hearing." The core of this story is her change of heart toward Pablo, which is revealed in the last lines.

I wanted to thank Pablo before Mr. Evans took over. I wanted him to know that his tomato was ripening.

Not every short short needs to end as "neatly" as Dalia's story. You do, however, want a conclusion that surprises the reader but at the same time makes him feel as though everything in the story was leading up to it.

You may think the ending is at fault when the problem may be that you didn't set it up earlier by hinting at what's to come. The end is usually not the place to introduce a character, detail, or action that hasn't already been alluded to or mentioned.

Sometimes, the problem with the ending is that there isn't any problem. It's the rest of the story that feels weak. If this is the case, use the last line as a "trigger" and work backward while timing yourself in a five-minute exercise. This isn't as difficult as it sounds. You're not "literally" going backward. You're just using the ending as a jump-off point. Ask yourself this question: What has to happen in this story in order for it to end this way? Don't think about the answer. Just write.

A SAMPLE REVISION

Here is an early draft of Morison Gampel's story. Following it are comments made by the class when he read it aloud. The revised story resulted from these comments. You need not agree with all the changes made. Keep in mind that this is not the only possible way to revise this story.

SECRET
(early draft)

She was a busy woman constantly striving to manage a growing family and a business—(both home and business) in one large but inadequate room.

She resented the demands of the little boy. One day she said to him: Now you be quiet and listen. Alright? Now I'm going to tell you something nobody else will know. Only you. Are you listening? He nodded eagerly. And she emphasized once again, Nobody else will know. And he smiled. And she whispered into the little boy's ear. Then she looked earnestly into the little boy's eyes. He smiled gratefully in acknowledgement and he hugged his mother. And he felt like a big man.

Now his mother proceeded to prepare the family dinner. The stove was hot, pots filled with familiar recipes were filling the large room with wonderful odors. And the table was being set and the little boy helped as best he could, shifting plates around, lining up the cheap silverware.

Later his brother and father appeared and they were very hungry and soon, around the table there were boisterous boy sounds intertwined with the parents' earnest recounting of the day's business activities. Everyone ate and talked with gusto. At one point, his older brother stopped eating momentarily and uttered aloud the very secret the mother had whispered in the little boy's ear.

The little boy was stunned. He was hurt but wasn't able to say anything. Of course, the family continued eating. It was just another meal. But the little boy's heart was pounding as he pretended to eat the delicious meal which was now tasteless. He felt betrayed but simply didn't know how to cry out his pain.

He kept his feelings of hurt to himself. Locked up in his being. And there they remained. Now he too had a secret. A real secret. One he couldn't share with his mother.

In this account of childhood betrayal, the point is clear: The little boy ends up having a secret, but not the one he wanted. While the point has nothing to do with the content of the mother's whispering, leaving it out makes it seem too important. By making the reader wonder what it is, this unknown information diverts attention from the focus of the story, which is the effect of the secret on the boy. Revealing the secret toward the end helps wrap up the story.

The following problems arise from unclear writing, incorrect grammar, awkward constructions, and needless repetition. The word *busy* is unnecessary: *constantly striving* implies this. We assume the mother is telling the boy a secret so he will stop annoying her. What specifically does he do to annoy her? What demands does he make?

Her spoken words should be contained by quotation marks. The future tense *will know* is used where the present tense is needed. *And* and *now* are used too often or misused. The word *emphasized* tells rather than shows. To be "grateful" *is* to acknowledge. The active verb *to prepare* is weakened by the auxiliary verb, *proceeded.* Pots are not "filled with familiar recipes"; they are filled with food. "Wonderful odors" sounds vague. How does the food smell? The words *business activities* seem too formal, out of tone. His brother doesn't need to stop eating to tell the secret.

The last two paragraphs need to be compressed. In the next-to-last paragraph, the first two sentences seem to carry the same weight. This neutralizes the effect of both. I would choose the first sentence because *stunned* sounds more dramatic. There's also repetition: "He was hurt but wasn't able to say anything," "He . . . didn't know how to cry out his pain," and "He kept his feelings of hurt to himself. Locked up in his being."

Here is the revised story.

SECRET
(revised draft)

She was a woman constantly striving to manage a growing family and business in one large but inadequate room. She resented her little boy, who always wanted her to play with him.

One day she said, "Now you be quiet and listen. Alright? I'm going to tell you something nobody else knows. Are you listening?" He nodded eagerly. Then she said once again, "Remember, nobody knows what I'm going to tell you." She whispered in the little boy's ear. Then she looked earnestly into the little boy's eyes. He smiled gratefully and hugged his mother. He felt like a big man.

After this, his mother prepared the family dinner. The stove was hot. From pots filled with food, made from familiar recipes, came fragrant odors, which filled the large room. While she set the table, the little boy helped as best he could, shifting plates around, lining up the cheap silverware.

When his brother and father arrived, they were very hungry. At the table, the boys' boisterous sounds mingled with the parents' earnest talk of the day's events. As they talked and ate with gusto, the older brother casually mentioned that his mother had won a hundred dollars in the lottery—this was the very secret the mother had whispered in the little boy's ear!

The little boy was stunned. Of course, the family continued eating. It was just another meal. But the little boy's heart was pounding as he pretended to eat the tasteless dinner that a moment ago had been so delicious. He felt betrayed, but he kept his feelings of hurt to himself. And there they remained. He had a real secret now. One he couldn't share with his mother.

REVISION AND THE WRITING PROCESS

My student Julie is good at getting the whole story down in five minutes. Her first revisions, however, usually stray far from the original exercise. She tends to add unnecessary details and make changes where none are needed. Only later, after further revisions, is she able to return to the original story with a new clarity. Like Julie, you may find yourself far from your original exercise. You may feel uncomfortable for a while, but this isn't bad. Wherever you are at any particular time in your story is the right place for you to be. Don't struggle against it. Don't rush or force yourself to finish. Accept wherever you are as part of your writing process. The quicker you do so, the quicker you'll be able to move on.

To make writing as pleasurable as possible, give yourself what you need. Use whatever writing instrument you prefer, whatever kind of notebook or paper. Write in the place that you prefer at the time of day that suits you best. Above all, allow yourself the freedom to play and experiment.

PART II

THE EXERCISES

SIX

FIVE-MINUTE FICTIONS

On the following pages you will find over three hundred verbal exercises. Most of them are randomly arranged in sets of six. I say "randomly arranged" though I was careful not to place what I consider to be similar topics too close together. Of course, my associations are not the same as yours because they're based on different life experiences.

For example, "Write a story about something that was stolen" is listed right above "Write a story about a party." If reading these two exercises reminds you that your or your wife's mink coat was once stolen at a party, you will naturally link these two. That's okay. You may need to write about this experience in order to get rid of it. Next time, when you use the same exercises again, you will be open to new associations. In other words, you do not want to limit yourself to writing only things that "actually" happened. What you want to do is free your mind so you can allow the unexpected.

The point I am making is this: You may not find that a particular set of exercises gives your mind maximum play, which is my intention. Especially in the beginning, it is important to give yourself as wide a range of subjects to write about as possible. Later, if you like, you may limit yourself to a particular topic, but for now, I suggest using as many of these exercises as you can.

If you have the time, do an entire set at one sitting. Don't stop to read each one before going on to the next. Just set the timer and go. The first exercises can be used as warm-ups.

Keep in mind that the exercises may be used to write both short short stories and longer fictions, which are written part by part. Parts are usually not stories in themselves, which is why I draw this distinction, but you will learn more about this when you read the third section of this book. All you need to know now is that when using the exercises to write parts of a long story or novel, you will use them without the words *a story*. For example, instead of "Write a story about a lie," you will simply "Write about a lie."

Below I offer some suggestions for choosing exercises. As you read this book, you will find more games you may play. Feel free to make up your own. There is a purpose to these games beyond your mere amusement. They keep your mind open, keep your mind moving so you can tune in on parts of yourself you may rarely bring into play.

SOME SUGGESTIONS FOR CHOOSING EXERCISES

- Write the exercises in the order in which they appear.
- Point to a set with your eyes closed.
- On each page of exercises, close your eyes and point to one exercise. Mark the exercise and keep going until you have pointed to six.
- Choose the set that interests or excites you most.
- Choose the set that interests you least.
- Choose a set that feels neutral.
- Write the sixth exercise in each of six sets randomly chosen.
- Write the first exercise in each of six sets randomly chosen.
- Write six different stories using the same exercise.
- Choose a set that contains at least one exercise you don't feel like writing.
- Look through these pages and choose the six exercises you find least interesting.
- Use these exercises in combination with the other verbal and visual exercises presented in this section.

Write a Story About . . .

Write a story about a lie
Write a story about something that really happened
Write a story about an animal
Write a story about an object that has been lost
Write a story about leaving
Write a story about a wish

Write a story about a broken promise
Write a story about something that was stolen
Write a story about a party
Write a story about something that hasn't happened yet
Write a story about a child
Write a story about a secret

Write a story about finding something unexpected
Write a story about someone you don't know very well
Write a story about a traumatic event
Write a story about a coincidence
Write a story about air
Write a story about a family

Write a story about food
Write a story about a reward or a punishment
Write a story about water
Write a story about a misunderstanding
Write a story about greed
Write a story about something wide

Write a story about two people
Write a story about hunger
Write a story about a trip
Write a story in which a person is performing a simple action, such
    as pouring coffee or riding a bicycle
Write a story about sickness
Write a story about something big

Write a story about madness
Write a story about arriving
Write a story about seeing something ugly
Write a story about a plan
Write a story about desire
Write a story about a conversation overheard

Write a story about falling
Write a story about seeing something beautiful
Write a story about money
Write a story about a heavy object
Write a story about memory
Write a story about sadness

Write a story about being trapped
Write a story about a place as seen by a woman in love
Write a story about a storm
Write a story about a shape
Write a story about climbing
Write a story about rage

Write a story about the sun
Write a story about friendship
Write a story about a wound
Write a story about being in a foreign place
Write a story about a flower
Write a story about sisters

Write a story about a crime
Write a story about a color
Write a story about death
Write a story about a dream
Write a story about something narrow
Write a story about flying

Write a story about an end
Write a story about a window
Write a story about pain
Write a story about something that is about to happen
Write a story about someone very different from you
Write a story about dancing

Write a story about the dark
Write a story about mountains
Write a story about shoes
Write a story about a sound
Write a story about something outrageous that happened
Write a story about a taste

Write a story about a game
Write a story about fire
Write a story about a book
Write a story about something you don't know
Write a story in dialogue
Write a story about trust

Write a story about a place as seen by a depressed person
Write a story about a chair
Write a story about being afraid
Write a story about hatred
Write a story about something that is not going to happen
Write a story about something you want that isn't good for you

Write a story about something old
Write a story about an idea
Write a story about something broken
Write a story about lust
Write a story about music
Write a story about an imaginary place

Write a story about smoke
Write a story about a painting
Write a story about something you see
Write a story about a tree
Write a story about something you can't see
Write a story about fish

Write a story about being young
Write a story about a smell
Write a story about an article of clothing that is really about
   something else
Write a story about someone dangerous
Write a story about a snapshot
Write a story about a city

Write a story about a toy
Write a story about a building
Write a story about something new
Write a story about a voice
Write a story about love
Write a story about something soft

Write a story about a delay
Write a story about a house
Write a story about envy
Write a story about magic
Write a story about innocence
Write a story about a symbol

Write a story about war
Write a story about a surprise
Write a story about something worthless
Write a story about harmony
Write a story about a car
Write a story about a revelation

Write a story about a building
Write a story about clouds
Write a story about something of value
Write a story about a texture
Write a story about a body part
Write a story about a message

Write a story about a beach
Write a story about stairs
Write a story about a stone
Write a story about warmth
Write a story about something small
Write a story about rain

Write a story about a lake
Write a story about a lesson
Write a story about a song
Write a story about a foreigner
Write a story about a letter
Write a story about dirt

Write a story about a neighbor
Write a story about selling
Write a story about a victim
Write a story about a meeting
Write a story about fame
Write a story about a loss

Write a story about a spy
Write a story about a wedding
Write a story about evil
Write a story about a hike
Write a story about a train ride
Write a story about a church

Write a story about an accident
Write a story about a smile
Write a story about an office
Write a story about shame
Write a story about a relative
Write a story about an enemy

Write a story about a wink
Write a story about a scream
Write a story about a celebration
Write a story about a school
Write a story about a yawn
Write a story about a pact

Write a story about a trial
Write a story about fur
Write a story about an argument
Write a story about faith
Write a story about a whisper
Write a story about waves

Write a story about an affair
Write a story about a factory
Write a story about losing
Write a story about thirst
Write a story about a champion
Write a story about forgiveness

Write a story about a friendship
Write a story about a gift
Write a story about wind
Write a story about a scream
Write a story about boredom
Write a story about cleanliness

Write a story about a train ride
Write a story about a sandwich
Write a story about a shooting
Write a story about a phone call
Write a story about a disguise
Write a story about a dinner

Write a story about a room
Write a story about a cough
Write a story about skin
Write a story about an omen
Write a story about an insect
Write a story about a drive

Write a story about a chant
Write a story about a sign
Write a story about disappointment
Write a story about an addiction
Write a story about laughter
Write a story about a speech

Write a story about gluttony
Write a story about weakness
Write a story about a divorce
Write a story about a decision
Write a story about uncertainty
Write a story about control

Write a story about a prayer
Write a story about a habit
Write a story about a grudge
Write a story about a celebrity
Write a story about camping
Write a story about a teacher

Write a story about playing
Write a story about light
Write a story about staring
Write a story about humility
Write a story about snobbery
Write a story about a performance

Write a story about drinking
Write a story about shadows
Write a story about chaos
Write a story about pretending
Write a story about shopping
Write a story about deceit

Write a story about a lawyer
Write a story about a coward
Write a story about a joke
Write a story about a hat
Write a story about something sticky
Write a story about metal

Write a story about hair
Write a story about a musical instrument
Write a story about a grave
Write a story about smoking
Write a story about snoring
Write a story about wood

Write a story about a jewel
Write a story about noise
Write a story about a doctor
Write a story about an island
Write a story about a farm
Write a story about remorse

Write a story about a prison
Write a story about a kingdom
Write a story about understanding
Write a story about stars
Write a story about sex
Write a story about running

Write a story about a risk
Write a story about a liquid
Write a story about strength
Write a story about a voyeur
Write a story about cheating
Write a story about bones

Write a story about tears
Write a story about a massage
Write a story about bitterness
Write a story about release
Write a story about a face
Write a story about failing

Write a story about tickling
Write a story about fat
Write a story about a store
Write a story about a tour
Write a story about garbage
Write a story about a test

Write a story about a tease
Write a story about a cure
Write a story about something invisible
Write a story about resignation
Write a story about space
Write a story about a plan

Write a story about a hole
Write a story about selfishness
Write a story about a mineral
Write a story about discomfort
Write a story about a witch
Write a story about a feud

Write a story about a rogue
Write a story about a holiday
Write a story about a fantasy
Write a story about a demon
Write a story about dread
Write a story about hunting

Write a story about a fake
Write a story about a riddle
Write a story about a rule
Write a story about a battle
Write a story about a souvenir
Write a story about a scar

Write a story about a trick
Write a story about endurance
Write a story about hope
Write a story about revenge
Write a story about sin
Write a story about relief

Write a story about a will
Write a story about glass
Write a story about a disaster
Write a story about a view
Write a story about something trivial
Write a story about a rite

USE EACH SENTENCE SOMEWHERE IN YOUR STORY

Use the exercises below after you feel comfortable writing those in the previous section. You may find these a little bit harder. Each of these sentences may be used at the beginning of a story, at the end, or anywhere in between. Like the others, these five-minute exercises should be timed.

It was a big house with two rooms.

I watched him staring at my cousin.

She lived alone, miles away from any other human being.

After several hours, we stopped for lunch.

He's not normal.

"I don't need anyone to protect me," she said.

They walked away without saying a word.

When he looked, it was gone.

He was uneasy.

She turned white—dead white.

He put down his glass.

My father was away.

She had her suitcase with her.

He is a very clever man.

"You'd better come now," they said.

She closed the door behind her.

I glance at my watch.

The sun had just set.

I lay down, but did not even close my eyes.

I laughed silently.

Won't he be surprised, she thought.

After dinner, they went into the garden.

She heard familiar footsteps behind her.

My father said no more.

The sky was stained crimson.

I went home after this.

She recognized him at once.

I too left the room.

One thing kept running through her mind.

If only she had known.

When he opened his eyes, he was amazed.

I now knew the reason why she acted this way.

The trail came to an end.

The little dog started barking.

SEVEN

SEEING STORIES

This chapter presents ten photographic images to be used in five-minute exercises. At first glance, you may find nothing especially promising about them. Why these images? you may ask. But for our purposes, this is not the important question. These exercises are not "about" the pictures. What is important here is learning how to use them to explore the richness of your mind. Think of them as tools. They can be a potentially endless resource. They are gateways into your unconscious if you allow them to be. You may even find that those images that seem least interesting to you trigger the most energetic writing.

Focus your mind on the image rather than on your thoughts about it. Whether you like the picture or not is beside the point. Learning to focus is the important part. But when you focus your attention on the photograph, don't try to stop your thoughts. Just allow them to pass through your mind.

You will find several questions accompanying each image. Your stories need not answer these questions. They are there to help you generate material, nothing more. If you want to generate stories without them, go ahead.

Don't worry if your stories have little or no relation to the photos. For example, if the seagulls remind you of your brother's parakeet, that's fine. If the man with closed eyes triggers a story about a trip to Sweden or the day your sister got married, go ahead and write whatever material your unconscious yields. Like the verbal directives in the previous chapter, these images need not be taken literally. Be sure, however, to time them as you have the others.

Do not spend time studying the photos before you do the exercises. You want to think about them as little as possible. Turn to an image, look at it for no more than a few seconds, read the questions (or not), set your timer, and write. You may use these images over and over to write completely different stories. Later, those of you who are particularly responsive to visual stimuli may create a file of images of your own. If you respond more to visual cues than to verbal ones, it is important for you to recognize this as part of your writing process.

Photo 1—Glove on stairs

Who dropped this glove?

Where was it dropped?

Was it dropped intentionally? If so, why?

What was the person thinking about at the time?

Where was the person going?

Where was the person coming from?

Was this person alone? If not, who was with this person?

Does the person ever find the glove? Why or why not?

Was this glove important to this person?

Does someone else pick up this glove? If so, for what reason?

Where is the other glove?

Photo 2—Chair

Whose chair is this?

Who else has owned this chair?

Where is this chair?

Why is this chair outside the house?

What happened to the last person sitting on this chair?

What did that person see while sitting on this chair?

What was that person thinking about while sitting on this chair?

Would someone else like to own this chair? Why?

What will happen to the next person sitting on this chair?

Will someone take this chair inside? If so, for what reason?

Will this chair be sold? Given away? If so, why? To whom?

Photo 3—House

Whose house is this?

Where is this house?

Who lived here before the people who live here now?

Who was born in this house?

Who died in this house?

Who was happy in this house?

Who was sad in this house?

Who couldn't wait to leave this house?

What happened in this house?

What is happening in this house?

What will happen in this house?

Photo 4—Boy on street with flowers

Who is this boy?

Where is this boy?

What is his family like?

What is he looking at?

What is he thinking about?

Who does he work for, selling his flowers?

Who buys his flowers?

Whom does this boy love?

Whom does this boy hate?

What depressing incident has happened to this boy?

What extraordinary event will happen to this boy?

Photo 5—Flying seagulls

Where are the birds going?

Where have the birds come from?

Are the birds hungry?

Who sees the birds?

Where is the person seeing the birds? On land? On sea?

Is more than one person seeing the birds?

What is being said about the birds?

What is being thought about the birds?

Is anyone frightened by the birds?

Is anyone annoyed by the birds?

Is anyone awed by the birds?

Photo 6—Island

Where is this island?

What happened on this island?

What is unusual about this island?

What is hidden on this island?

Who sees this island?

What was lost on the island? By whom?

What was found on the island? By whom?

Who visited the island?

Who was disappointed by the island? Why?

Who was amazed by the island? Why?

What will happen on this island?

Photo 7—Woman with hand on mouth

Who is this woman?

Where is this woman?

What is she thinking about?

What happened to her?

Why is she touching her mouth?

Is she hiding something? If so, what is she hiding? From whom?

Who is looking at this woman?

What does the person looking at her know about her?

What lie has been told about this woman?

What lie has this woman told?

What will happen to her?

Photo 8—Doorway

Where is this doorway?

Who just left the building?

Who just entered the building?

Who made a date to meet someone in this doorway?

Who waited for someone in this doorway who didn't show up?

Who made a deal in this doorway?

Who fell in love in this doorway?

Who had an argument in this doorway?

Who found a friend in this doorway?

Who cried in this doorway?

Who laughed in this doorway?

Photo 9—Man with closed eyes

Who is this man?

Where is this man?

What is he thinking about?

What is he feeling?

What are his dreams?

What are his fears?

What are his hopes?

Whom does he love?

Whom does he hate?

What happened to him?

What will happen to him?

Photo 10—Office

Whose office is this?

What kind of work is done here?

What unusual transactions take place here?

Who worked in this office before the present occupant?

What kind of work was done previously?

Is the person working here honest or dishonest?

What worries the person working here?

What surprising calls does the person make?

What surprising calls does the person receive?

What happened in this office?

What will happen in this office?

PART III

WRITING LONGER STORIES AND NOVELS

EIGHT

GETTING STARTED

In the preceding sections of this book, you have used the five-minute method to generate an entire story in one exercise. In this section, you will use the method to write a story or novel part by part or exercise by exercise, which is different from what you've been doing thus far. You will probably find it easier because the only limitation is the five-minute one. As in previous chapters, I will use work of my students to illustrate key points.

USING THE FIVE-MINUTE METHOD

Whereas a short short story reveals a situation or moment in a flash, a longer fiction or novel takes place over time, so you don't have to compress your material, and you don't have to rush to get everything down in one exercise. You don't need to have an ending or an epiphany. Your exercise need not be surprising or complete.

Wherever you are at the end of five minutes is fine. You can always do another exercise and begin from the place where you left off. In fact, you can do as many exercises as you need to complete your longer fiction. In each exercise, you have the freedom to say as much or as little as you please.

An exercise for a longer fiction may not be able to stand on its own and still have meaning. It exists for the sake of the whole. For example, instead of telling a story, it may present background material, introduce characters or a setting, establish a mood or a point of view.

You may, however, continue to generate an entire story in each exercise if that's what you want to do. You have that option. You may link short short stories that have, for example, a common theme, or the same cast of characters, or a common voice, or the same setting, but this is a special way of working and will not be specifically addressed.

Instead, the focus of this section will be on showing you how to create a continuous story or novel by writing in five-minute bursts. The time limit will force you to focus and concentrate your energy. I will show you how to get started with or without a plan. By the end of the next chapter, you will have begun your first draft, like my student Stephanie Dickinson has done in the example below.

Her first exercise does not read like a short short. It does not tell a complete story. It does not get to the core incident. Instead, she has used the five minutes to introduce two of her characters and establish the point of view and the quirky voice that belongs to Velma, a "fortyish woman" who likes younger men and sells fishing equipment on the pier of San Luis Pass. She will drug and kidnap Robbie, a handsome young "half-Cherokee, half-Cajun oil worker." His educated, "somewhat prissy" girlfriend, Cynthia, will find him some days later in Velma's quarters and try to assault her, but Robbie will come to Velma's aid. Here is how Stephanie begins.

> She's sick of it, sick of rolling another fishing pole across the counter at another beer-fat Mexican or German down from Friedricksburg. If she has to wiggle another rubber worm or handle the flab of a squid, the lavender jelly flecked with brown moles leaking down her forearms, she'll go crazy. Maybe she is crazy. She's ugly that's for sure.
>
> Well, there's trouble, she thinks, looking over the kid fisherman who swaggers in. She gapes at his bare chest, with curly black hairs ringing his nipples. He doesn't see her. He just sees the wiggle worms. She's seen him before. Sure enough. He's the one.
>
> "What can I do you for?" Velma says, using her tough voice.
>
> "I want your freshest dead shrimp."
>
> "All my dead shrimp are fresh."
>
> "Bull. Smell my hands," the man says, wiping his fingers on the back of his cut-offs.
>
> A full moon falls over the black water and Velma feels the white trout coming in like silvery scoops of spooked cream.

In chapter nine, I'll show you how to proceed step-by-step to write your first draft. In the final chapter, I'll show you how to pull it all together and refine it.

You will find this method helpful if you like to proceed with caution. Consider each five-minute exercise a small step forward. You're less likely to get overwhelmed and anxious if you take one step at a time. If you tend to get stuck, if your ideas dry up, if your energy runs out, or if you live in fear that one or all of these will happen, the strategies presented in the next chapters will help you in spite of your fear.

If not having time is your problem, consider writing six exercises a week. That will take thirty minutes. On average, each exercise will probably be at least a page in length, though I wouldn't be surprised to find some considerably longer. Let's say every other week instead of writing new exercises, you do a minimum of revision on the ones already written, based on the questions in the following pages. Over the course of a year, even if you throw out half your exercises, you'll be surprised at how much work you have done.

You do not, however, need to have a problem to appreciate this method. You may be a writer who just likes to try something new. If so, have some fun and enjoy it.

STARTING WITH OR WITHOUT A PLAN

You may start your longer fiction with or without a plan. Like Luisa Valenzuela, some writers never work from a plan. They believe that knowing their stories in advance would kill the energy in their writing or, at the very least, limit what they have to say. They are sparked by the adventure, the surprise that is part of the writing process.

Other authors find planning helpful. Patrick McGrath wrote his first two novels without a plan, but for his third, he made a detailed plan, and said that working from it cut his writing time in half.

Try both methods if you like. Then choose the one that feels most comfortable to start your longer story or novel.

GETTING STARTED WITHOUT A PLAN

Let's say you want to write something longer, but the thought of writing longer fiction still seems overwhelming and scary. In your fear there is energy, which is all you need to start. The fact that you want to begin something longer may be a sign that you already have an idea or direction in mind even if you're not consciously aware of it.

The First Exercise

You will be choosing your first exercise from the same list in section two of this book that you used to write short short stories. When you read the directives that begin "Write a story about," eliminate the words *a story* in your mind, since you're no longer limited to writing an entire story in each one. This means that you will change the directive to "Write about . . ." In section one, I defined a story as a container for change. But in a longer fiction, something doesn't have to change or happen in every exercise.

You are free to write your story part by part. A part may be a passage of description, a statement of fact, an opinion, a memory, a digression, a page or two of dialogue. It may also be written in the form of a letter, fable, diary, monologue, confession, or treatise. Even a recipe can be a part of your fiction. It is whatever you write in five minutes.

The exercise you select will be as easy to write as those you have written for short short stories, unless you allow the logical, rational side of your mind to interfere. Allow yourself to be led by your unconscious. Allow yourself to write spontaneously. If you try to figure out beforehand what will happen, if you search your mind for interesting, original, or clever ideas, if you try to say something "important," you will defeat the purpose of the exercises.

You do not need "important" ideas to write a longer fiction or novel. I don't know of any novelists who start novels because they have "important" ideas. They start novels because they have the urge to write something longer, just as you do.

You don't have to know anything special to start. You don't need years of study and preparation. At this point, all you need are exercises. This is not the time to worry what your novel will be about. *Everything you need to know you will learn in the process of writing.*

The long fiction or novel is a staircase with many steps. Imagine those steps lost in the clouds. You can see only the first one, and right now that is the only step you need. You are not trying to imagine the others. Trying in any way will interrupt the process.

Before you start, remind yourself that whatever you write is okay, even the silliest, most nonsensical things. Remember, you may do as many timed exercises as you like until you find one that feels right. No one else has to see what you've written. Your exercises are just for you, so allow them to go where they will.

Take a deep breath. Relax. Clear your mind. Now set the timer. Choose an exercise at random. Any one at all. Don't think. Just write. You're not trying for a masterpiece. You're not even trying for something good. In fact, you're not trying. You're not doing anything but writing. You're not thinking, planning, or evaluating. If you slip up and find yourself reading the exercise before the timer goes off, let yourself go back to writing.

Okay. Five minutes are up. This is the time to read and evaluate the exercise, but as you already know, the evaluation I am speaking about has nothing to do with judging the writing as good or bad. What is important is judging whether or not you are excited or interested by your words. How you *feel* about them is important.

Look at what you wrote. Does it excite you? Are you anxious to write more? How would you rank it on the energy scale? If, on a scale from one to ten, you rate it at six or above, you may assume that you have made a start. Keep setting the timer and writing exercises until you have one that excites you enough to rate high on the scale.

Let's say you have written a five-minute exercise you have rated at seven. How do you know if this work is the beginning of a longer fiction? After all, an exercise is only a five-minute burst of energy. How do you know if you have enough to say to write a novel? At this point, you don't know. But you have a piece that excites or interests you sufficiently to want to take it further; it gives you a feeling of possibility.

What Happens Next?

Okay, you have the first exercise. Now what? The easiest way to continue is to reset the timer and ask yourself the following question: What happens next? It's that simple. Then write your second exercise. If it also feels exciting—six or above on the energy scale—ask this question again. If you find yourself with three exciting exercises, you have probably begun your longer fiction or novel. Remember, every exercise you write in answer to this question may not feel inspiring. But if you get three out of eight, for example, I'd say you're doing fine. Hemingway once said that he liked to stop working at a point where he still had something left to say. That way he could continue with a sense of excitement the next time he sat down to write. Like Hemingway, you don't want to exhaust yourself in one sitting. It's a good idea to stop writing *before* your energy runs out.

Write About . . .

The straightforward strategy—What happens next?—is not the only way to generate exercises. Instead, you may choose additional directives from the list in section two, as long as you eliminate the word *story* from each directive (unless you're writing a long fiction made up of complete short shorts). The single sentences and photographs in section two may be used as well.

How you choose the directives is up to you. Have fun with this process. You may choose one with your eyes closed, for instance, or you may choose the third directive in each of three sets. Any way that works is fine. My student Jon likes to write the exercises on scraps of paper, which he folds and drops in a jar. After shuffling them, he picks one at random. He says this keeps him from thinking about each topic when he reads through the list. (For more ideas on choosing exercises, see section two.)

What you say in the exercises, however, is far more important than how you choose them. When writing a new exercise, keep in mind the one that came before. Don't dwell on it. Just be aware of the time and place, the characters, the circumstances, the point of view. The relation between one exercise and another is unimportant when using them for independent short shorts, but in a longer fiction or novel, they must connect in some way. Without trying, you will probably find yourself using at least some and perhaps all of the elements in your first exercise. In other words, it's very likely that without conscious effort, the same characters, setting, conflict, and point of view will come up in exercise after exercise. Use each new directive to move your story forward.

My student Debbie Chapnick used random directives to write a long fiction that was based on an actual experience. It takes place on a blind date, arranged by her well-meaning friend Amy, during Debbie's visit to Texas, where she went to escape "all the disappointments she experienced in eastern standard time." Debbie's first exercise was "Write about a lie." The lie was not immediately apparent to me when she read the piece aloud. The exercise was triggered, she told me later, by her expectation that all cowboys would be like John Wayne, until she made a trip to the Lone Star State and found her idea of a cowboy was far from the truth.

You may have no idea why a particular directive sparked a particular exercise. In fact, what you write may seem totally unrelated to it. Remember, however, that unconscious forces are at work when you allow yourself to write spontaneously. You may never know what unconscious associations led you to write a particular exercise. What counts in the end is the writing, not *how* it came to be.

After dinner and a rodeo, the narrator's blind date in Debbie's story "shifts his hat to the back of his head" and suggests they go to a local bar.

> " . . . My best friend Buddy is waiting there for us. He wants to meet you."
>
> "Sure," I replied. I had just watched grown men feel a sense of accomplishment roping a small defenseless calf. I was ready for anything. "Why does Buddy want to meet me?" I asked.
>
> "Buddy likes to meet all my blind dates. If he thinks you're okay, you are. Buddy's a great judge of character."

She chose "Write about leaving" for her next exercise, but this directive plays at most an indirect role. The real trigger seems to be the sentence "Buddy likes to meet all my blind dates." She starts off like this.

> All his blind dates? What had Amy done to me? Was this man a career dater? Did she think we'd get along or was she just trying to show me how good my life was until now?

She says that in the smokey bar "there wasn't a head without a cowboy hat on it." Buddy yells when he sees them.

> "Over here!" He had a bottle of Lone Star in one hand and his hat in the other. I knew he had a pick-up truck with a gun in the back seat.

The third exercise was "Write about finding something unexpected." Here, Buddy's girlfriend seems to be the unexpected find. It begins when Buddy kisses the narrator's hand.

> I didn't want any part of my body to come in contact with the beer foam dangling from his mustache.

She says this about Buddy's date.

> She was the blondest woman I had ever seen, by choice, not by birth. . . . Her hair cascaded down her shoulders, mixing with the leatherette fringe on her vest. God, what did he say her name was? I should have listened but the visual had grabbed all my attention. I shook her hand carefully, trying to avoid any damage from those ruby red nails.

As Debbie has shown, there is no right or wrong way to use the directives as long as your exercises have energy and connect. If your exercises don't connect, you may prefer this next strategy.

Writing From the Exercise

Your exercises will connect naturally if each one is generated by the one before. Debbie used this method inadvertently when she chose the sentence "Buddy likes to meet all my blind dates" to trigger her next exercise.

Look closely at your first exercise. It may have bad grammar, words to cut, sentences to change, but revision is beside the point at this moment. Right now try to pinpoint the energy. The energy may be concentrated in a sentence or two that stir you, in a phrase, an image, or an idea that is only alluded to. Focus on the part that moves you, interests you, or may even upset you, then underline it, and use it as the inspiration for your next exercise.

Donald Corken used this method to generate the first draft of his story "The Answering Machine." He started with an exercise from the list of directives: "Write about a wish." Then he allowed the sentence with the most energy to trigger those that followed. Included here are parts of Donald's exercises and the sentences he used as springboards.

> He was sitting by the phone, wishing it would ring. He had interviewed at the company three times, and he really thought he had a good chance of getting the job. "Call me, call me, call me," he said out loud. "Call me!" *He had already gone out on two unnecessary errands, hoping that when he returned, he'd see*

the red light flashing on the answering machine. Both times there was no message, even though one time he stared at the machine for over a minute, hoping that maybe when he blinked he had missed something. Instead, the machine mocked him by not turning on its red light. . . .

Donald used the sentence in italics above as a springboard. In other words, by focusing on this sentence for a moment, he was able to free-associate and continue his story.

He tried to think of another reason for going out of the house. Should he call a friend to have lunch? *He ruled that one out—he didn't have any appetite because his stomach was in knots, and he knew he'd be too cranky to be very pleasant company.* A walk around the block? That would take about ten minutes, but that might just be the ten minutes it would take to get the call.

He went back out, and said the name of the man he was waiting to hear from, softly but urgently, under his breath, like a chant, with each step. "Da-vid. Da-vid. Da-vid." He tried some visualizing techniques a friend had taught him. Imagine David at his desk, he thought, looking for my number, finding the number, reaching for the phone, dialing the number, my phone ringing. . . .

The sentence in italics above was used as the trigger for the next five minutes of writing.

He was back at his front door in less than ten minutes because he had walked unusually fast. When he got back to his apartment, there was a blinking light. A call! He played it back. "Hi, it's Stephen. Just called to see if. . . ." He turned it off before it finished. He knew Stephen was calling to see if he wanted to have lunch or something. He suddenly hated the sound of Stephen's voice. He hated Stephen. As a friend, shouldn't he know not to call him on a day when he was expecting a life or death phone call? *He wanted to smash the machine, or throw it out the window.*

This last sentence inspired the next exercise, which begins as follows.

Instead, he picked up a magazine and threw it as hard as he could at the wall over the couch . . . startling the cat out of her nap. She looked at him resentfully, and jumped down. . . . "What do you want from me?" he hollered at her, but then he felt guilty. . . .

And so Donald's story continues.

In addition to using parts of your exercises as springboards, you may also invent your own directives. Let's say this sentence holds the most energy: "She wondered how he could fail to notice the change in her hair color." You might give yourself one of these directives: "Write about her hair color" or "Write about why he doesn't notice the change in her hair color." However you phrase it is fine as long as it inspires you.

In an exercise that feels exciting, it may be difficult to pick out a specific part that has the most energy. There may, in fact, be several different parts or elements or ideas that excite you. If that happens, choose any of them to use as a springboard.

If, after doing several five-minute pieces, you find your energy and enthusiasm building, you have probably made a start. You may need to write a number of exercises, however, until you come up with three or four that excite you.

When you have written three or four exercises to use in your first draft, make a list of lesser elements, including characters, actions, images, and thoughts, that also spark your interest. You may find these lesser elements in some of the work you chose to discard. They may be useful in later exercises, especially if your energy begins to flag.

If, in the second or third exercise, you find yourself losing your excitement after focusing on the most exciting element, change your focus. Concentrate instead on something in the exercise that is mundane, a sentence or phrase or image perhaps. Or pick a random sentence or phrase and focus on it. See what it sparks.

Have fun with this process. It should not be a rigid routine. One day my student Naomi complained she was really excited by what she was writing and then suddenly the time was up, so she forced herself to stop. I mention this because the exercises are not meant to be straitjackets. They are just tools to keep you "cooking," to trigger your writing. If you are really excited by an exercise and have more to say, keep going. Allow yourself to vary your strategies. Allow yourself to abandon this method at any time.

GETTING STARTED WITH A PLAN

You may choose to start your longer fiction with a plan, but if you do, it's important to remember that whatever plan you make may change in the course of your writing as new ideas, new characters, new situations, or new scenes arise. If you are inflexible, you will face the frustrating task of trying to "fit" things into a fixed plan.

By a plan I mean a scheme or design for your longer fiction, a way of arranging the parts so that the story or novel works as a whole. A plan allows you to see the emerging shape of your fiction. It provides a view of the whole before it is written. The best approach is one that is allowed to grow or change over time. Writing is organic. It is alive. If nothing else, the five-minute method demonstrates just how alive writing is. The process of making a plan can be as alive and spontaneous as the process of writing exercises. In this chapter, you will have the opportunity to see just how spontaneous a working plan can be.

Plan One

Plan One is basic. In fact, you can't get more basic than this. All you have to do is answer the following questions:

1. How does the story start?
2. What happens in the middle?
3. What happens at the end?

Remember that in a story or novel, there is a problem or conflict that builds to a climax and gets resolved in some way at the end. Keep in mind that most of the drama occurs in the middle. So you may want to sketch in key scenes or events.

Now that you've read all three questions, go back and read the first one again. Then start writing. You don't have to set the timer. Just write as quickly as you can. You may write an idea you've been thinking about for a long time or you may use these questions to generate something new. Don't think about your answers; just write whatever comes up.

You may use complete sentences, the way Patty McCormick has done below, or fragments or phrases that are unintelligible to anyone but you. Do whatever feels right. When you finish the first question, go to the second. When you finish the second, go to the third.

The idea Patty chose for her novel is one she has thought about for quite a while. She has even done some research on this project. Here are Patty's answers just as she wrote them.

How does the story start?

> *A young girl, frustrated that she has no role to play in the Civil War, is drawn reluctantly into the underground railroad.*

What happens in the middle?

> *She harbors a runaway—her own age—so they get to know each other and realize that they are not that different. Her courage is tested when a bounty hunter becomes suspicious of her.*

What happens at the end?

> *The girl foils the bounty hunter and guides her new friend to safety. The war ends—her family shattered—but the runaway is safe.*

You have a basic plan for a story if, like Patty, you have answered all three questions. That plan, however, is useless unless it has energy. If you're not excited by what you wrote, answer the questions again. Change the plan until you feel excited by it. When Patty reread what she wrote, she decided the word *shattered* was too strong in the third response and substituted the word *changed*. Don't be afraid to alter your original words. Words are not sacred because they are spontaneous. Don't be afraid to try out different ideas. Don't be afraid to play. Have fun. Use these questions to see where your energy is. You want your plan to have as much energy as your exercises.

Okay, let's say you know how the story starts, what happens in the middle, and what happens at the end. Here are four more basic questions to answer that will help you see the shape of your longer fiction.

1. Who is telling the story?
2. Who are the characters?
3. Where and when does it happen?
4. Over how long a period of time?

The answers to these questions may already be contained within your plan. If so, you need only draw them out. If not, you need to answer them directly before you go any further.

Patty answered the questions like this.

Who is telling the story?

> *Meg, a fifteen-year-old tomboy.*

Who are the characters?

> *Meg, Mother, slave, bounty hunter, teacher, dog, Luke and Tom.*

Where and when does it happen?

> *In a small Pennsylvania farm town, from May 1863–1865.*

Over how long a period of time?

> *Two years.*

When you've answered these questions, go back to your basic plan and pick out the word or phrase with the most energy in your answer to the first question. Use that word or phrase as the inspiration for a five-minute exercise.

In Patty's first answer, she felt excited by the word *reluctantly.* Here is the exercise she wrote.

> The danger was enormous. She knew that harboring runaways was against the law. There was a $500 fine—even a jail sentence—for anyone caught helping fugitive slaves. But hadn't her mother told her it was her Christian duty to help those in need? True. But she'd also said it was "pure folly" for a few people to try to overthrow slavery. Well, she would steer clear of this band of undergrounders. Good people come to bad ends by taking the law into their own hands. She would simply tell Luke and Tom she wanted nothing to do with their band of lawbreakers.

Will Patty actually use this paragraph in her novel? Maybe. Maybe not. In any case, it has given her a place to start. If she chooses, she may pick out the word or phrase or sentence with the most energy in this exercise and use it as a springboard for the next. She may continue to use this method until she has three to six exercises that excite her. Or she may abandon the five-minute method and just keep writing until she slows down or gets stuck, at which time she may once again pinpoint the exciting word or phrase or sentence and use it to generate her next burst of writing. Never at any time feel that you must stop just because five minutes are up.

More Plans

Instead of using Plan One, you may answer a set of questions under one of the following headings: "Pick a Character," "Pick a Problem," "Pick an Incident," or "Pick a Setting." You may, in fact, try all four. You may use the same character in all four sets, for example, or you may use the same problem, the same incident, or the same setting. Each set of questions will give you the opportunity to see the same thing from a different point of view. In a story or novel, the elements don't operate exclusively—you can't separate character from problem from incident from setting. But you can emphasize one over the others; you can focus on one element at a time.

Review the four sets of questions below and choose one of the headings. Read each question, but do not stop and think about each one. Jot down the answers quickly. A word or phrase may be enough. If not, write a paragraph. How much detail you include is up to you. You don't, however, want to waste your best writing in a summary or sketch, so don't belabor your plan. Stephanie chose "Pick a Setting" and answered the question "What is the setting?" as follows.

> San Luis Pass, a cut-through channel to the Gulf of Mexico. It is a fishing beach with a pier. The beach is desolate, with sand dunes and a surf of black water. The beach is known for its white trout and sailtop catfish and draws blue collar fishermen. There are warning signs in the shallows that read "Dangerous Current."

My student Claire, however, answered the same question like this.

> A bar.

If you hesitate over a question, skip it and go to the next. You don't have to answer every question the first time around. You can go back over your plan when you finish. If you have gaps or you're not satisfied with your answers, don't be afraid to start over, but do your rewrites and make your changes quickly. Be sure to answer the question "What excites you about . . ." In the exercises that follow your plan, this question may help you focus on the part with the strongest energy.

Pick a Character

If you have several main characters, you may use this set of questions for each one.

1. Who is the character?
2. Where is the character?
3. What is the character's problem?
4. What excites you about the character?

Pick a Problem

1. Who is having the problem?
2. What is the problem?
3. Where and when does it take place?
4. What excites you about this problem?
5. How is the problem resolved?

Pick an Incident

You may use this set of questions for every incident in your story or novel.

1. What is the incident?
2. Where and when did it happen?
3. Who was involved?
4. What excites you about this incident?
5. What is the outcome?

Pick a Setting

1. What is the setting?
2. Who are the characters in this setting?
3. What happened in this setting?
4. What excites you about this setting?

After you answer the questions, put them aside. You are ready to start doing exercises. This time you will do something a little different.

You will set the timer for five minutes. Rather than focus on any particular answer in your set, you will write whatever you want about your chosen character or problem or incident or setting as long as it relates to your plan. Even if the exercise doesn't strictly follow your plan, don't discard it. As long as your exercise has energy, you're on the right track.

To generate your second exercise, you will pinpoint the sentence or phrase in the first one with the most energy and use it as a springboard. You will do the same to generate the third.

You do not have to tell the whole story in the first set of exercises. Remember, you are writing a longer piece of fiction; you are writing part by part. A longer piece unfolds gradually. Susan, who is accustomed to writing short shorts, chose to write her exercises about a problem, but complained after doing them that she never got around to writing about the problem described in her plan. The class disagreed after hearing what she wrote. Susan's first exercise begins like this.

> Peter sat on the couch watching the TV with vacant eyes. He felt stifled in this room. Had it always been this small? With his wife sitting on one side of him and his teen-age daughter on the other, there was no chance of escape. He knew that they were no more interested in the figures prancing on screen than he was, they were just there to protect him.

In subsequent exercises, Susan shows the man feeling more and more trapped. He wants to escape, but his wife and daughter won't leave him alone for a second, not even to get a soft drink from the kitchen.

After hearing her exercises, I asked Susan to tell me the problem she had chosen. She said the man was suicidal. I told her she had evoked this suicidal man very well. I thought she had a strong beginning. She had created a situation that was tense, claustrophobic, and intriguing.

In class, Morison also chose to write a plan about a problem. In his plan, a man suddenly falls on the street and is helped by a friend. Afterward, the man who fell doesn't know what happened. But Morison felt that he answered the questions "wrong." He felt that the fall didn't qualify as a problem, though no one in the class could understand why he felt that way.

It's important to remember that there are no right or wrong answers in your plan. There are only answers that have energy and answers that do not. If you rate your exercises at six or above on the energy scale, you've made a start, even though your exercises may not fit your idea of what you think you *should* be writing. If only one or two exercises rank high on the energy scale, do more until you have three or four with sufficient energy.

It took writer Kim Connell only a few minutes to write this plan about a problem.

Who is having the problem?

> *An alcoholic college English professor.*

What is the problem?

> *The police are looking for him. He killed his wife accidentally in a blackout.*

Where and when does it take place?

> *Upstate New York, early 1990s.*

What excites you about this problem?

> *Will he turn himself in or commit suicide?*

How is the problem resolved?

> *Suicide.*

Kim generated the following five-minute exercise from his plan.

> He looked out the bar's dirty window at a police car that was stopped for a traffic light. His pulse racing, he gulped his scotch, ordered another. The sun was setting, casting a pink glow on the dirty snow shoveled to the edge of the sidewalk. Finally the light changed, and the police car drove on. He sighed, *wondered what motel he could stay at.* He couldn't go to any friend's house because in the small town the news had spread quickly.

The second exercise was generated by the sentence in italics.

> The night before he had stayed at a Motel 6 because he could park his car behind the building so it wasn't visible from the road. He'd given a false name, paid cash.

He sipped his drink, lit a cigarette. *He could either call a lawyer or get on the Interstate and leave the area.* With the $12,000 he'd withdrawn from the bank, he could go to another state and get a new social security number and go to work as a carpenter. Could he get a teaching job? Perhaps, but he would have to be clever.

The sentence in italics above was the springboard for his third exercise.

He was careful not to go faster than 60. Pennsylvania was just a few miles down the road. The stream of car headlights flashed by. In the dark, his brown Chevy Citation was just another car, but when he passed a cop car hiding behind an overpass abutment, his pulse quickened.

Was he really doing this? Leaving a good prestigious job for a totally new life, never to see any of his friends again and the large old farmhouse he'd renovated himself?

If convicted of manslaughter, how many years could he get?

Kim's exercises have energy. If you find that yours don't, or if you find yourself losing interest in the character or problem or incident or setting, choose another idea or another angle and start again. The goal here is to create a character or problem or incident or setting that sparks your interest enough to write a longer fiction or novel.

Do not go to the next chapter until you have written at least three exercises that excite you. Do not write more than six to start. If, while writing, you have one or two exercises about events that happen at a later point in time, put them in a provisional order. These exercises provide a destination even if you're not sure how to get there yet.

NINE

GOING BACK AND GOING FORWARD

I had a student named Lynn when I first started teaching. She was a skilled and imaginative writer who worked on her unplanned novel in small spurts. She would write a scene, revise it until it was perfect, then she would go on to the next. The scenes were not written in chronological order. She wrote each one as it came to her. The problem was that she refused to look back at the scenes she had written before going on to the next. While she was writing, I tried to persuade her to arrange the scenes in a provisional order so she could see how they worked as a whole. Reading them together would give her an overview, I said, and would enable her to see the gaps in the novel and the places where it still needed work. For example, issues such as needless repetition, unwanted shifts in tone, and, most important, lack of a climax or high point would have become apparent when comparing one scene with another.

Lynn, however, was reluctant to do this because she had suffered from writer's block in the past and was afraid that if she took a step back and was critical of the piece as a whole, the five-minute bursts of writing that came so easily would stop. She could overcome her "critic" while writing in five-minute segments. She could even revise individual exercises to perfection, but she was unwilling to look at the larger work. She thought that "somehow at the end the parts would all fit together" like pieces of a puzzle. This magical thinking didn't work. Each part was beautifully crafted, but together they didn't make up a whole. By the time Lynn allowed herself to see this, however, she had written two hundred pages of "perfect" prose. At that point, the idea of reworking each part seemed overwhelming, and indeed much of it would have been tedious. At this juncture, Lynn decided to give up.

I tell you this sad tale—I'm still hoping Lynn will change her mind and finish the novel—to impress upon you the importance of going back over your exercises as you write. You may not feel like doing this, but I urge you not to let your feelings win out.

When you have written six or so exercises that rank high on the energy scale, it's time to take stock of what you've written, unless you are like my student Chris. He is one of those writers who feels compelled to keep going. He starts off with a five-minute exercise, but finds that he has just begun when the time is up. It's part of his process to write around twenty pages without stopping. When he finishes twenty pages, however, he reviews what he has written.

Like Chris you may not need to stop every time you have six exercises. You may end up writing for fifteen minutes rather than five, or you may stop when you have four or eight more exercises rather than six. You may vary the process to suit yourself. Whatever you do, however, be sure to review your work often. Reviewing as you write could make the difference between writing two hundred pages of a cohesive novel and giving up in the middle. Even Chris, who works by instinct and feels sure of his direction, finds characters that are underdeveloped or scenes that go on for too long.

THE PROCESS OF GOING BACK

It may sound a little crazy to begin going back when you have barely gone forward, but I think you'll see it's not as crazy as it seems. It's easy to go on and on, to do one exercise after another and, like Lynn, hope they will turn out to be the story or novel you want. Even if you pick out the exercises that excite you and discard the ones that don't, there's no guarantee the remaining parts will work without some help.

Choosing exercises with energy is only the first part of the process. The second part is going back over your writing to find or make a structure for whatever you want to say. The structure is the overall order of the work. In the following pages, I will show you how to find or make that structure.

See Your Exercises as a Group

Whether your story or novel is planned or unplanned, you will shape it as you write. Each time you finish six or so exercises that rate high on the energy scale, step back and review them as a group. This allows you to see how one relates to another.

It may be helpful to imagine yourself in an airplane looking down at your exercises. See them together. Hold them in your mind. How do they look? Do you see them lined up horizontally? Or are they stacked one on top of another? The shape may be vague, half-formed. My student Dave saw his exercises defined by an outline of dots, not all of which were connected. Julie saw a series of squares. Imagine any shape you like as long as you see it containing all of your exercises. Allow that shape to change and expand as you write.

Ask Questions

The questions I pose in this chapter will help you see weak spots in both the structure and story line. Asking questions will be particularly useful if you sense that something is wrong, but you're not sure what the problem is, or you know the problem, but you're not sure what to do about it.

Skim the questions below as you go back over your exercises. But before you do, read this entire chapter. Each question is discussed at some length under the heading "What to Look For When You Go Back."

- Are your exercises connected? If so, how are they connected?
- Are you satisfied with the progression of your exercises?
- Is the point of view working well?
- Will your beginning grab the reader?
- Does too much or too little happen at one time?
- Have you established a frame? In other words, do things happen in a particular time and place?
- Have you introduced a conflict?
- Have you created tension?
- Are there unwanted shifts in voice, tone, rhythm, or distance?
- Do important parts have more weight than lesser ones?
- Do some parts move too slowly or too quickly?
- Does one incident lead to another?

- Are there holes in the story?
- Is there needless repetition?
- Does the conflict reach a high point?
- Have you found the right ending?

Keep Your Exercises Unfinished

In the early stages, you're concerned with working out the story line and finding or making the structure. Later, you'll have plenty of time to go back and perfect every word. By keeping every exercise unfinished, you give yourself the freedom to play, to explore. In this way, you keep yourself open to new ideas as they come. So allow your revisions to stay rough. *The more attached you are to your words, the harder it will be for you to change them.*

In the early stages, you don't care if your exercises are beautifully written. In fact, if they have less than beautiful writing, they'll be easier to change. You want to be able to cut parts that are superfluous or add parts where you find holes, but you aren't concerned at this point with finding "the right word." You aren't concerned with writing fluid sentences. You aren't even concerned with changing the order of paragraphs within a particular exercise unless the order changes the meaning of the whole.

It may be difficult to keep yourself from fussing over each exercise, but the less you fuss the better off you will be. You may end up keeping very little of what you write the first time around. Polishing exercises in the early stages will probably be a waste of time.

See yourself as an explorer at the start of a journey. See yourself staking out virgin territory rather than putting down roots, because you're still not sure where you're going or how you're going to get there.

WHAT TO LOOK FOR WHEN YOU GO BACK

When you write five-minute exercises, your unconscious takes over, but when you review, you bring into play the critic inside you as well. If you inadvertently shift your story from first to third person, for example, as my student Abby did, you want to be able to recognize and correct your mistake. You want to be able to look at what you've written and improve upon it where you can.

In a story or novel, everything is connected. For example, you can't separate point of view from conflict when you write, but you can separate them by asking questions when you go back over your exercises. The questions, which I listed earlier, are examined in this section at some length. They will enable you to recognize and focus upon specific common problems so that you can work them out.

Are Your Exercises Connected?

When you review your exercises, ask yourself, Are they connected? Are they part of the same story or novel? Is there a thread running through them? The thread could be a common theme or the same cast of characters or the same situation, conflict, mood, or voice. If you're not sure, list the elements they have in common. They may have one or more of the above. If they don't, you may have six interesting exercises that have little or nothing in common. You don't want to start a story or novel with several totally different ideas. Keep in mind that exercises may be connected in a nonlinear way like those written by my student Julia. Her exercises flow back and forth in time, but they're linked by the adult voice of the narrator looking back on different parts of her past.

If you don't find a connecting thread, or one that feels strong enough, choose one of the six pieces and pick exciting sentences to use as springboards, or use the "Write about . . ." directives to generate five more. You can avoid the problem of finding a connection, however, by directing yourself from the start to write about the same theme, characters, or events in all your exercises. Alison, for example, came up with a character named Dr. K., a man who believes he can cure all disease. Whatever topic she used to generate her exercises, she used Dr. K. or one of his patients as her subject.

If you can't find a connection between your characters, but don't want to discard them, make something up. Are they all rocket scientists? Former Nazis? Childhood friends? Just for the fun of it, try connecting the characters in several different ways. Make up an event that will bring them together. Maybe they meet on a cruise ship. Maybe they meet at a séance. Use your imagination. Write for one or two minutes to add "connective tissue" to your existing exercises or write completely new ones. You may hint at the connection between characters rather than stating it outright. In fact, discovering the connection between them could be what sustains the reader's interest.

Gail described her six exercises as "going all over the place." But she knew the thread running through them, or so she said. She thought the narrator was the thread because the characters were part of her large family. Each exercise presented different relatives taking part in different incidents at various points in time. For instance, one piece described the wedding of one of the narrator's cousins. Another recounted an argument between the groom's parents and the narrator's husband. Still another described the funeral of the grandfather. And so on. Gail was not as sure about the thread once she gave it some thought, so I asked her to make a chart. This would help her see what happened first, what happened second, and so on. It didn't matter at that point whether she wanted to tell the story in chronological order or not.

The chart helped her organize the material. Arranging the exercises in sequence helped her see what she still needed to write. In other words, she said to herself, "This exercise goes here, then there's a big space I have to fill in, then comes this exercise, then comes another big space, then comes another exercise," and so on. In the spaces between exercises, I asked her to list the topics she wanted to cover and to put these in chronological order, too. On her list were topics such as Cousin Maud's party, Frank's heart attack, Irma and Joel's disapproval of Heddy. After she made this list, which was still far from definitive, I asked her what else tied these characters and incidents together. She said their religion. All of them had definite beliefs about Judaism. The narrator's conflict was whether or not to go against her family by not following the orthodox faith. Once it was clear that religion was the real thread, it was easier for her to see which characters and incidents were necessary. Gail saw this while making a provisional order for her exercises.

Are You Satisfied With the Progression of Your Exercises?

Place your exercises in a provisional order as Gail did. If you are not sure what connects your exercises, seeing them in order may at least give you a clue. Keep in mind that the thread you are looking for may be nothing more than *a feeling* at this point.

Play with the order. What happens when you change it? Choose the sequence that *feels* right. Keep in mind, however, that the order you start with may not be the one you keep. In fact, you may change it every time you add six more exercises.

The order you choose doesn't have to be chronological, but if you don't have another plan in mind, it's the easiest way to organize your work. You may as well give it a try. It's not, however, the only way to proceed. You might choose instead to base the order on alternating viewpoints. For example, character A might tell the story in the first few exercises, while character B might tell the same story in the next few exercises.

Or you may find your story contains several throughlines happening at the same time. In other words, different strands of the same thread may run parallel. If this is the case, you might create a regular pattern in which one story consistently follows another. For example, if your novel is composed of three stories, you might have story number one in the first exercise, number two in the second, number three in the third. In the fourth exercise, story number one would continue, and so on. Or you might allow numbers one, two, and three to randomly weave in and out.

Is the Point of View Working Well?
The first time Liz arranged her exercises in chronological order, they felt disconnected, but she didn't understand why. It took her a while to realize that her point of view was inconsistent. She was writing a novel about a girl growing up. Some exercises were written from the child's viewpoint. Others were written from that of the adult remembering childhood. Liz had to make a choice. Writing from the child's point of view would limit her to seeing the world through the child's eyes only.

> Last night the girls in my cabin got naked and gave a fashion show. No clothes, just naked bodies.

Writing from the adult's point of view would allow her to write about childhood and growing up, but the viewpoint would not be from the child's perspective.

> My best friend was Nadine. When she was ten, she was a tall pine tree of a girl.

Donald suggested changing the point of view gradually from the child to the adult. In other words, the narrator would age with the girl in the novel. Joanne suggested using an all-knowing narrator, one who could know things about the girl that even she could not know. The girl's story could even be told through the eyes of her sister or brother or her best friend, Nadine. Or it could be shown through the eyes of two or more of these characters. In the end, Liz chose to keep the original narrator and gradually age her from childhood.

The point of view was also inconsistent in Peter's story, but his problem was a little different. His longer fiction is narrated by a son whose father is killed when the truck he is driving blows up. The son recounted details, however, that only someone at the scene of the explosion could have known. Since in the original exercises the son was nowhere near the scene, Peter had to decide whether to change the narrator to an all-knowing one or to place the son at his father's side. Since he felt comfortable telling the story from the son's perspective, he decided to have the son accompany his father but narrowly escape his father's fate.

Telling the same story from different points of view can be challenging. If you decide to use two narrators as Donald did, be careful not to change the viewpoint in the middle of a scene. Change it only when you start a new one. In Donald's novel, Brian, a young gay man who rents a room in Joan's large apartment on the upper west side of Manhattan, sees the world from a humorous and slightly ironic point of view, whereas Joan, an older woman, is world-weary and cynical.

If your story is told by two characters, make sure each has a different voice, different thoughts, and a different way of seeing the world. To write in the voice of a character, you have to become that character. Try to imagine *being inside* each one's skin. Here is Donald writing from Brian's point of view as Brian walks down Christopher Street in Greenwich Village for the first time.

> He noticed the men passing in their tight jeans and construction boots and their plaid shirtsleeves rolled up just so. Then he noticed his own reflection in the store windows—tall and scrawny, in baggy khakis and penny loafers and a thrift store shirt. Could any one of these muscular men with their neatly trimmed mustaches view him as an object of desire?

Here is Donald writing from Joan's point of view.

> Joan walked into the too brightly lit restaurant, and waited
> for the hostess, as the sign posted inside the door advised.
> "Hostess" seemed an incongruously elegant word, considering
> the type of restaurant it was, Joan thought.

The angle from which you tell your story is basic. If you're not
sold on the point of view you're using, experiment. Try out different
viewpoints. Analyze how each one changes your story. Rewrite your
exercise in first-person, third-person, omniscient, or multiple points
of view.

If you write about a wedding, for example, the bride's father will
see the wedding differently than the jilted cousin who wanted to marry
the groom. You may also try rewriting your exercise from the viewpoint of a detached observer or a character who is deeply involved. A
mother will see her sick son from a different perspective than the
nurse who is taking his temperature. You may also experiment by
putting your story or novel in past or present tense. You may find, for
example, that you prefer present tense because it gives more immediacy. Whether you choose one or more viewpoints, make sure you
stick with whatever you choose.

Will Your Beginning Grab the Reader?

In one of Alison's stories, the narrator's father has just been rushed
to the hospital. From the start, the story focuses on the question: Will
he survive? But Alison doesn't state this directly. Here is her first
sentence and part of her opening paragraph.

> When she arrived at the hospital, the first thing she saw was
> dirt, dirt everywhere. . . . The walls were covered with grime.
> The floor looked sticky. . . . How could they bring her father to
> such a place? . . .

The reader soon learns that her father has suffered a heart attack.
He's had other heart attacks. The prognosis doesn't look good. The
dirtiness of the hospital doesn't improve his chances. Had there been
time, the narrator says, her father would have been admitted to a
clean, decent hospital, but this one was nearby. She describes bloody
tissues, dust motes on the floor. She becomes obsessed with the dirt,

which is easier to face than the fact that her father might die.

Look over your exercises. Have you chosen a beginning that will pull the reader in? Ask yourself if you have created *a hook*. An unusual voice, a surprising statement or question, an unusual point of view may stir the reader's interest as much as a dramatic event.

Does Too Much or Too Little Happen at One Time?

Marie touches upon a number of characters and situations in one exercise. She introduces Shawn and his buddy Roddy, both carpenters fresh from Ireland, who have come to New York to start a new life. Marie describes Shawn and Roddy's first days in the city. In the same exercise, Matilde, a woman who loves Shawn, arrives from Ireland, and Shawn's great-uncle, long dead, comes to him in a dream of warning. He says that Roddy has some bad habits Shawn should know about. Also described is the great-uncle's role in the siege of Leningrad and his later move to South America, where he became a mountain guide.

There are a number of potential scenes in this one exercise. One scene might present Shawn and Roddy's first days in New York, for example. Other possible scenes might explore Shawn's friendship with Roddy, Shawn's relationship with Matilde, Shawn's great-uncle, Shawn's dream, Roddy's bad habits, or even the past they fled in Ireland.

Look at your exercises. Where have you placed the most characters and incidents? Have you crammed a bunch of them in one or two exercises? Count the number of characters and incidents in each one. If you have overloaded an exercise as Marie has done, make a list of characters and a list of incidents or potential incidents. Star or underline ones that can be explored later in more detail. Pick no more than two or three characters and a single incident and write a five-minute exercise.

When you have a number of characters and incidents together in an exercise, you can't say much about each one, but when you go back, you have the opportunity to examine the characters and the incidents in depth. Allow yourself to develop those few characters or expand one incident into more exercises. Save the other characters and incidents, introducing them gradually over time.

The problem in your story or novel may be that too little is happening instead of too much. If you spend pages describing every piece of furniture, for example, in a house with twenty rooms, the reader will lose interest long before you reveal the point of this inventory, assuming there is one. Readers resist a world that feels static. They need to feel that the story or novel is taking them somewhere. Static moments work best when contrasted with moments of action. Listen to your exercises on tape. Ask yourself, Is there too much description? Is there too much explaining? Is there too little action?

Have You Established a Frame?

Charles wrote a story narrated by a junkie who has been recently released from a detox clinic. It begins some time after the junkie has accidentally run into the woman he loves. He hadn't seen her since she left the clinic a couple of months before him. In despair, the junkie, who is back on drugs, says she held a red rose in her hand, probably a gift from a lover. Reading this, I wondered how much time had passed between the incident and the junkie's narration of the incident. Writing a coherent story from an incoherent viewpoint is no easy task. If he were really high, the story would have needed another narrator, but Charles assured me that the junkie knew where he was. This brings me to another problem: The reader didn't know *where* the junkie was when he was telling the tale.

The frame is the *when* and *where* of a story or novel. Time is one element that establishes the frame; setting is another. Sometimes writers leave out the frame and write only the inside of their stories. In other words, they write only the action or event and fail to provide the time and place. To prevent this, ask yourself, When do my exercises happen? Do they all take place within the same time frame? You may want to ask yourself how much time your story or novel will cover. Will it happen in a day? A week? A month? A year? The frame gives shape or structure to your story and allows you to work within it. It limits a narration that may be potentially endless and formless.

The reader may also be thrown off by leaps in time, which are likely to create holes in your story. Look at your exercises. Will the reader wonder how much time has lapsed between one event and another? For example, if a few months have passed between events, you will probably need to bridge the gap. That bridge may be as simple as adding "A few months later" or "A while later" or "Three days later." In this way you provide a transition between a few days or even a few minutes. If you skip a longer time period, you may need to summarize events before you go on. Look at your exercises. Ask yourself how much time is covered in each scene.

Once you've established the time frame, ask yourself *where* your story or novel takes place. Your exercises may occur in different settings. If the location changes, make the reader aware of the change. If your exercises don't have a setting, the reader is likely to feel she is "floating" through your narrative. A story without a frame or one in which part of the frame is missing makes the reader feel ungrounded, unable to catch hold.

Charles intended his story about the junkie to take place while the junkie is walking down the crowded streets of midtown Manhattan. Having the city's sights, sounds, and smells intrude on the junkie's memories from time to time was just what Charles needed. The physical details, such as bumping into a pedestrian or nearly getting hit by a car, contrast with the junkie's inner monologue and place him within a frame so that the reader can hold on to his thoughts.

Have You Introduced a Conflict?

In fiction, something is wrong. There is a question that needs to be answered, a problem that needs to be solved. There are opposing forces. Tension results. The conflict gives rise to the action and builds to a climax or high point.

The conflict may be internal. One character may be of two minds. Imagine a teenage girl who wants to sleep with her boyfriend immediately as much as she wants to wait until they marry. Whenever a character harbors opposing attitudes or drives or beliefs, she is in conflict.

The conflict may be external. One character may oppose another character or group or nature itself. A girl may be in conflict with her mother. A leader may go against his gang. A sailor may oppose the sea.

In a longer story or novel, you don't have to introduce the conflict in the first few sentences or even in the first exercise, but if you've written a number of exercises and you still haven't found a conflict, make one up. The easiest way to do this is to choose two characters and imagine them in disagreement with each other. Ask yourself about the nature of their disagreement. Why are they at odds?

As you go back over your exercises, try to describe the conflict in one sentence, based on what you've written so far. Putting it into words may help you focus.

Have You Created Tension?

If there isn't any conflict, there isn't any tension. In Alison's story about the father with a heart attack, tension builds as the daughter waits in the dirty hospital to see if her father will live or die. But what, you may ask, builds tension in a novel like Donald's tale of the gay man, which doesn't pose life-or-death questions? What keeps the reader turning pages?

In truth, there wasn't much tension in Donald's first fifty pages, so I asked him to tell me in one sentence what the novel was about. He said it explores the relationship between Brian, a young gay man who is trying to find himself, and an older woman named Joan, who rents him a room in her apartment. I said his answer was too vague. What is important about this relationship? What is the conflict in this novel? Donald described the conflict like this: When Brian and Joan become close friends, Joan intrudes upon his life and tries to stop him from being independent. When I asked Donald why there wasn't a clue in fifty pages that the novel was heading in that direction, his reply was that he was still "setting things up."

Sometimes the writer is reluctant to let the story out. He may write two hundred pages and still not *get to* the story. There's a lack of tension because the writer is marking time. There's also a lack of focus. Donald's novel had a tendency to follow a pattern: He did this, he did that, he did this, he did that. The writing was flat because nothing stood out. None of the characters' actions seemed to serve any purpose. If your exercises lack tension, write in one sentence what your story or novel is about. Rewrite that sentence until it captures the main conflict. Keep this nearby. Refer to it often.

In one of Donald's exercises, Joan has a fight with her boss. She's in danger of being suspended from her job. Instead of using this incident as an opportunity to create tension, however, Donald at first passed it by. In this scene, Joan tells a co-worker that she doesn't care if she's suspended because she's waiting for a transfer to a different office. It was Alison who pointed out the possibilities he had missed in that scene.

In Donald's revision, Joan is still in danger of losing her job and she still tells a co-worker that she doesn't care, but this time Donald lets the reader in on the feelings Joan keeps hidden. He reveals her fear of losing her pension. He shows her berating herself for yelling at her boss. Donald poses the same question as before: Will Joan lose her job? But this time, Joan has something at risk. There's more reason for the reader to care.

The ongoing problem in a novel is how to keep the reader's interest. A novel needs tension, not only in the beginning, but all the way through to the end. If you lay all your cards on the table, there's nothing more for the reader to find out. To create tension, which is a state of psychic unrest, one or more characters must have something at stake.

In Donald's novel, Joan's argument with her boss is an example of a minor complication, which is useful for creating tension. To set up a minor complication, ask a question, leave something unsaid, or withhold a piece of information to keep the reader guessing.

Diane, for instance, has her character Susan slip a postcard from Australia into her pocket so that her husband Michael doesn't see it. The reader doesn't learn who sent the postcard and why until later in the story.

When you withhold a piece of information, don't forget about it. Be sure to reveal it in another exercise. In some cases, you may want to wait until the end.

Another tactic for creating tension is to hint at something that will happen in the future. Here's a sentence from Joanne's story.

> If Alice could have seen the consequence of giving Al her number, she never would have done it.

Use one or more of these tactics to create a hook in every group of exercises. Seduce the reader by not giving too much of your story away at any one time.

Are There Unwanted Shifts in Voice, Tone, Rhythm, or Distance?

If you write infrequently, if you take long breaks from your work, or if you skip around from one section of your story or novel to another, you're likely to find unwanted shifts in voice, tone, rhythm, or distance when you go back over your exercises. Try to direct your writing to one section at a time. That way you'll have more of a sense of how each exercise relates to the next.

Unwanted shifts are likely to occur when you lose the mood or "feeling" of your narrative. To avoid this problem, *read your existing exercises carefully before you continue writing.* Take the time and effort to get back inside your story, especially if you've been away from it for a while. Feel the spirit of it before you pick up your pen. You may need to be in a particular frame of mind in order to write. Allow yourself to go into that state. Take a deep breath and relax. See the existing exercises in your mind. Don't expect to automatically pick up from the place you left off. Writing without regard to your prior exercises will probably waste your time.

In Craig's story, "a lowly clerk" stalks a woman named Maggie who works in a nearby office. There's an angry edge in the clerk's voice when he talks about his job, but he softens as soon as he sees "his love." At one point, he decides that seeing her at lunchtime isn't enough, so he starts following her home on the subway. Hidden in nearby bushes, he watches her come out at night.

> There was something in her walk, something in the way she carried herself that was more free, more real. We were out of that phony world in Manhattan where you had to be someone you weren't or kiss somebody's ass. It was just the two of us now.

In his next exercise, however, that angry edge in his voice is gone. The clerk sounds "mushy" and romantic. The unwanted shift in voice causes the story to slacken.

> I could see her spending afternoons alone in her room, reading or looking out the window. "I know you can feel me, my love," I whispered outside the house. "I'm here my love, I'm here."

As you go back over your exercises, ask yourself, Do my exercises have the same voice? Voice includes everything from the vocabulary you choose to the perceptions of the characters and the ways they see the world. Look for inconsistencies. If the narrator uses slang in one exercise, for instance, but doesn't use it in another, there needs to be a reason why. If you don't have a reason, correct it.

It's easy to confuse tone with voice because tone, which is the attitude of your story or novel, is part of the voice. Changing the tone may be appropriate as it was in Sandra's story in which the narrator's husband has given up after losing his hand in an accident. The narrator starts out bitter, but by the end, she has a change of heart. After watching a stranger encourage his retarded son, she understands that her husband has given up in part because she has given up on him. This realization makes her feel almost hopeful about the future. Ask yourself if the tone changes in your story. If so, make sure there is a reason.

How can you be sure there are no unwanted shifts in voice, tone, rhythm, or distance? Read your exercises into a tape recorder. Notice if some parts sound emotional, for example, or if other parts sound flat. Listen to your word choice and to the rhythm of the sentences. Notice where you pause to breathe. Are you using words with many syllables or with only a few? Are your sentences fast in one section and slow in another? Are some sentences long and others short? Differences are not necessarily bad or wrong. It's simply important for you to recognize them and have them serve a purpose.

How close to you are the characters in your story? In one scene, you may be near enough to see a character's eyelashes and hear him whisper. In the next, you may see him on board a ship in the mid-Atlantic, a tiny figure leaning over the rail. Again, it's not necessarily bad or wrong to create shifts in distance—though abrupt shifts in distance may be jarring—but it's important to recognize when such shifts occur.

Do Important Parts Have More Weight Than Lesser Ones?

When every element in your exercises has equal weight, nothing stands out. Nothing feels important. Everything is levelled. Everything is *background*. When you go back over each group of exercises, pick out the single most important scene or event in each.

In Wanda's story, a live-in nanny named Jeannie works for a dysfunctional couple called the D.s and takes care of their little girl, Scotty. Jeannie's conflict is whether or not to leave her job. Mr. D.'s abusive behavior toward his wife reminds Jeannie of her own childhood. She detests both Mr. and Mrs. D., but she's grown attached to the little girl. In the end, she decides to stay because Scotty needs her.

The reader, however, doesn't realize until the middle of the story that Jeannie has been in serious conflict with herself over whether or not to leave. Until then, the reader is only aware of her dissatisfaction. Even when she makes up her mind, the important lines are buried in a paragraph in which smoking a cigarette has as much weight as deciding to leave.

> I got up really early, around 5 A.M., lit a cigarette and leaned out my window. Mrs. D. didn't let people smoke in her house so I had to smoke on the sly. This was the day I was going to do it. I would never have to pick up Scotty again. When I finished, I rubbed the cigarette out on the window sill, brushed the ashes into an envelope and stuck it under the mattress.

Jeannie goes on in this paragraph to cut and dye her hair. Later, however, when Jeannie is called upon to take Scotty to school because Mrs. D. has a black eye, she reconsiders her decision.

The first time I read the entire story, I overlooked Jeannie's decision to leave, so her decision to stay in the end didn't make much sense to me. The class decided the story should start with her decision to leave. That way her change of heart at the end would be more convincing.

> This was the day I was going to do it. I would never have to pick up Scotty again.

Wanda was able to emphasize these lines by changing their position. This is one way of giving more weight to a part that is important, but not the only way.

If the conversation between two guests at a dinner party is the single most important part of your exercises, you don't want to spend equal time talking about the other guests. I often find inexperienced writers giving too much attention to unimportant details and incidents. The main events are passed over in favor of those that are all but unnecessary. Ask yourself which parts are important in your exercises. Which is the *most* important part? Listen to your feelings. If you're still not sure, pick *something*. Later, you may change it, but by then you will understand how to mold or shape your exercises by giving more weight to one part over another.

Whatever part you choose, *amplify* it. Write more, expand upon it, go into it in depth by using the "Write about . . ." directives or the most exciting sentences or phrases to trigger more exercises. If you wrote one page the first time, try writing four or five pages. An important event may turn into a scene of many pages.

Give minor details and events less weight by giving them less space. Cut actions, events, descriptions, and explanations that neither advance the story nor develop the characters. If, however, you feel energy in a particular part and say to yourself, "Well, gee, I like that," try to connect it before you cut it. Every scene needs to be there for a reason. If you're not sure whether to leave something in, ask yourself these questions: What does this part add to the story? Why does the reader need to know this?

Look to see if you've explained an action you have also shown. If you show Mrs. Saunders throwing a frying pan across the kitchen, and then you say she is angry, you are showing and telling the same thing. Choose one.

When you give more weight to important parts and cut lesser parts or give them less space, you are molding your exercises. You are shaping your fiction. You may want to keep a list of important parts or key events as you write. The list may help you carry the story's shape in your mind and keep you from taking a wrong turn.

I often find that first novels using a chronological order wind up sounding like journals, especially if they use autobiographical material. The writer seems to think that everything Joe ever did needs to be included. There's no high point or climax. It just goes on and on.

The fact that the novel reads like a journal is not necessarily bad or wrong. A journal is one of many forms a novel may take. The problem once again is that everything sounds the same because nothing is emphasized, nothing is minimized. If equal weight is given to the scene where Joe stops to buy a newspaper and the scene where Joe is held at knifepoint by a gang, and this later event changes Joe's life, you need to amplify the pivotal scene and downplay the others. You would cut the newspaper scene entirely, for example, if it weren't connected in some way to the key event. If, however, Joe has a premonition that something bad is going to happen when he stops to buy the paper, that scene may be useful for building suspense.

Do Some Parts Move Too Slowly or Too Quickly?

Every piece of fiction has a special pace at which it develops. Sometimes it will hurry; sometimes it will slow down. In general, important events will be slower. They will be written as though the reader is there as they happen. There will be more detail. The reader will be able to linger in the scene.

A number of exercises may be necessary to complete a single scene that is important. Let's say you are writing about a son who is visiting with a mother who comes and goes in his life. He has conflicting feelings about her. In one scene, he opens a door and walks cautiously across a room to the chair by her side. In real time, this action might take a minute, but if you choose to tell the boy's thoughts and feelings as he walks across the room, you might write ten or even twenty pages. If, on the other hand, the three-month period the boy spent with his grandmother in the country is not important, you might summarize that in a single sentence. Less important events may be dealt with in less time.

Does One Incident Lead to Another?

In fiction, something happens because something else has happened. Every time you go forward and write six exercises, you may need to go back to adjust what you have written.

There are reasons why characters behave the way they do. Things happen to them, physically, mentally, or both. For example, if Tom hadn't been dumped by his first love, Betty, he might be more inclined to marry Hilda now. But if the reader doesn't know about Betty, the reader might not understand why Tom backs off.

Or if Tom likes Bill in one exercise but dislikes him in another, the reader needs to know what happened in between to change Tom's mind. Perhaps Bill persuaded Tom to invest in a shady deal in which Tom lost money.

In a novel, there may be many complications. Characters need motives for their actions. The reader needs to understand *why* they do what they do. When you're writing unplanned exercises and your characters behave in ways you didn't expect, you may need to go back and set up reasons for their actions in previous exercises. In other words, you may need to set up actions or events *after* they have taken place. It may be enough to provide hints or clues, or you may need to make more extensive changes. You may need to show, for example, how a character behaved in a similar situation in the past.

If, at one point, Bill slugs Marty in a bar, you need to ask yourself if Bill's action makes sense in terms of what you have told the reader earlier about the two men. If you've established that Bill is a hothead who holds grudges, it will be easy to imagine him hitting Marty, especially if you've introduced Marty as a lady-killer who stole Bill's girlfriend a few years back.

Are There Holes in the Story?

When you read your exercises in sequence, you may find holes, places that sound abrupt, choppy, or disconnected. You may be unable to follow the sequence of events. Something doesn't make sense. You may feel as though you're climbing a flight of stairs when suddenly you are stopped by a step that isn't there.

There may be holes in the narrative or holes in the action. A hole is any place where something is missing. The part that is missing may be seemingly small, a few words of transition, for example, but it may be vital to the reader's understanding.

A hole will occur when either part of the story line or part of the structure is missing. If you've left out the phone call Derek makes to tell Mona he is coming back, the reader will wonder why Mona isn't surprised to see a man she hasn't seen in fifteen years. This is a hole in the story line.

A transition establishes a link and moves the reader from one disparate part to another. When you leave out a transition, you leave out part of the structure. If you are writing a novel that tells two stories simultaneously, this link provides a bridge for the reader to cross when you shift scenes.

Even in places where a transition plays a minor role, its absence can feel jarring. In Wanda's story, there is a long telephone conversation between Jeannie, the live-in nanny, and her best friend, Bingo, also a nanny. Bingo says that Jeannie's employers, the D.s, were seen coming out of an all-night porn parlor. Suddenly, Bingo sees her employer, Mr. A., coming and has to hang up. Without pausing, Jeannie launches into a long narrative passage about the D.s. When Wanda realized that the reader has no time to adjust to the change, she added the following lines.

> I hung up the phone, and thought about what Bingo had
> said. In fact, I couldn't think of anything else. Why did the D.s
> go to a porn parlor? I wondered. . . .

This transition allowed Wanda to lead the reader slowly into Jeannie's narrative. You might wonder why something as obvious as Jeannie hanging up the phone has to be stated. It needs to be stated because there is a scene change here. A transition is like the neck connecting the head and the body. Without the neck, we don't know that the body belongs to the head.

Read your exercises into a tape recorder. Try to identify the places where the story stops. When you find holes, add a sentence or two of "connective tissue," or try writing mini-exercises by setting your timer for one or two minutes instead of the usual five.

Is There Needless Repetition?

You may find yourself repeating information from exercise to exercise because you don't know yet where each fits in the whole. In Wanda's story about Jeannie, each exercise presents a fragment of a different situation. As she was writing, Wanda didn't know what the order of these fragments would be, so she tended to repeat herself.

In one exercise, while Jeannie dyes her hair purple, she recalls a memory of her father. In the next exercise, Jeannie recalls another memory of her father. Since Wanda didn't know which exercise would come first, she wrote the second memory as though she hadn't already introduced him. She repeated, for example, both his physical description and the fact that he had abandoned her years earlier. These facts she repeated in a third exercise as well, this one about her mother's funeral, which was the last time she saw her father.

Exercises overlapped. Wanda would introduce something new about the father only after restating information she had already given somewhere else. This needless repetition kept the reader from getting a picture of him as a whole. The reader saw him only in overlapping fragments until Wanda pulled details about the father from each exercise and put them together in the following paragraph.

> At my mother's funeral, I couldn't stand looking at him: all
> skinny and smoking cigarettes like crazy in front of the funeral
> parlor, with that ugly grey crewcut and wearing that camouflage

T-shirt under his suit jacket. He came up to me at the cemetery and I freaked and started crying. He kept saying over and over, "I'm sorry, Jeannie, give me a break, give me a break." He stuck this piece of paper in my jacket pocket and walked away fast. When I got home and looked, all it had on it was a phone number with an area code. I looked it up, it was in Nevada. But I still haven't called.

When Wanda cut the repetition, it surprised her to see how little she had actually written. The repetition made her think she had written much more. When she saw the fragments together, she felt she could expand this scene. She decided to write more exercises about the father *and* the mother.

Repetition won't be a problem if you keep putting your exercises in a provisional order every time you have a new group. As soon as you put them in order, see what information, if any, has been repeated. It may be helpful to see the same material in different positions to determine the place where it works best. If you're not sure and don't want to cut any material yet, underline the repeated parts and come back to them at a later time.

Or try this. If you have three or four exercises repeating the same material, cut the repeated part from all of them. Either take that part and expand it into another exercise, or choose an existing exercise and reintroduce it. In the early stages, it doesn't matter much in which exercise you leave the repeated material as long as you leave it in one of them. Many of your exercises will change as your story or novel develops, so wherever you leave it at that point is probably not its final "home."

It may also happen that the duplicated material is so enmeshed in each exercise that you can't cut it without eliminating other parts of your exercises that you want to keep. If you have to cut more than you like, jot down the parts you want to save in a separate notebook or on a separate sheet before you cut them out.

If you find yourself retelling the same thoughts or ideas over and over, you're investing a lot of energy in those words. Try using them to trigger one or more exercises as Wanda eventually did. See what happens. When something keeps coming back, there's a reason. There's probably more to be said. This pattern may be your unconscious mind telling you this part needs attention. Not every instance of repetition, however, merits such scrutiny. Take a good look only at those segments that repeat time and again.

Does the Conflict Reach a High Point?

Debbie's cowboy story, as you may recall, takes place at a bar in Texas. There the narrator, an Easterner on vacation, has come with her blind date, Billy Bob, to meet his best friend, Buddy, and Buddy's date, Susie, a stripper from Lulu's Love Lounge. From the start, the storyteller and Buddy are not well suited. As the evening progresses, the tension between them grows. The lewd way Buddy talks about Susie arouses the other woman's anger. Buddy accuses her of being a feminist. He challenges her to prove to him that Susie's not a sex object. The narrator tries to defend Susie by saying she's an entertainer, but eventually gives up. When Buddy swings Susie's chair around and squeezes her breasts, however, Billy Bob's date decides she's had enough. She gets up and leaves. Billy Bob reluctantly follows. The high point comes when Susie, who has hardly spoken all evening, runs after them into the parking lot, yelling

"Were ya really gonna leave me in there alone with him?"

The narrator can hardly contain her surprise.

"You don't want to stay with Buddy?"
"Stay with him? I don't even know him."
"You're kidding," I said.
"He paid me $75 to pretend we were dating."

Buddy, too drunk by this time to chase Susie, leans against the bar door and screams at her to come back so he can get his "money's worth." His legs slowly give way. When Billy Bob tells his date he's going over to help Buddy, who has already collapsed on the ground, the narrator tells him he's wasting his time. Buddy can't fall any lower, she says.

In Debbie's original exercises, there were three key incidents. In the first, the narrator becomes so enraged by Buddy's comments about Susie's body that she loses control and starts screaming at him. In the second, Buddy squeezes Susie's breasts. The third is Susie's revelation in the parking lot. Each key incident occupied the same amount of space and was given equal weight. One was not more important than the others.

When she reread her exercises, it was clear to Debbie that Susie's revelation was the high point of the story, the culmination of everything that had taken place. A high point or climax may be an action or realization or both. It is the scene the reader has been waiting for.

To give more weight to the high point, Debbie expanded the scene in the parking lot and made the narrator's earlier argument with Buddy less intense; otherwise, the reader would wonder why she didn't leave sooner. The second key incident, Buddy's obscene behavior, is less important on its own in the revision and more important as the trigger for the narrator's exit. This is the incident that leads the reader directly to the climax.

See your exercises as a whole, and ask yourself if all the actions lead to a high point. If you can't find the climactic incident, go back over your exercises and list the key events. Pick one that happens near the end and amplify it by choosing the sentence or phrase with the most energy, or by using a directive from the "Write about . . ." list to trigger one or more exercises (more if you're writing a novel). Use them to expand the key event into a climax. Go deeper. Make it more important. You might even choose to make it more extreme.

Once you have a high point, go back to the beginning and adjust your story as you go forward so that every scene builds to the climax, or you may work backward from the key action or event to the cause. Allow yourself to have fun with this process. As you revise, ask yourself if each scene advances the story. If the answer is no, cut the scene or rework it. Don't be afraid to eliminate scenes, change them, or add new ones.

Sometimes one part of a story or novel is amplified merely by downplaying other parts. Susie's silence at the bar, for example, makes her behavior at the end more surprising. In retrospect, her silence makes sense. The fact that Buddy was paying for her company explains why she didn't defend herself against him and stuck it out for as long as she could.

Don't shortchange the reader by letting the high point pass too quickly. A paragraph or a page in a novel isn't enough. It took time and effort for you and the reader to reach this point, so make it worthwhile.

Have You Found the Right Ending?

The ending is the final outcome, no matter what the length of your fiction. In stories, the high point may also be the ending. This is true in Debbie's case. When the outcome takes place after the high point, however, as it does in novels and some stories, it usually happens *soon* after.

The outcome grows out of the story. After you read it, it seems inevitable, though it may not be the ending you or the reader had come to expect. If you're writing a novel, it's here that the plot winds down and the last loose ends are tied up. Though this is not the time to introduce anything new to the reader, the conclusion you draw may be a surprise.

If you have trouble ending your story or novel, start with the last line that has energy, set your timer, and write some exercises. You may write one-, two-, or three-minute exercises rather than the usual five. Keep doing them until you find one with energy. When you do, rather than refine it, let it stay rough, and put it aside for several days or more. When you reread it, see if it still works. As your story or novel develops, you may change the ending several times, so don't get too attached to the first one you find. Don't spend too much time on the ending until you have a sense of your work as a whole.

See the ending as the final stitches in the tapestry. These last stitches give the viewer the whole picture. Without them, threads would be left hanging or, worse still, the tapestry might start unravelling. You can make sure your fiction doesn't fall apart at the end by asking yourself some questions. Is it clear where and when the ending takes place? Are the actions at the finish consistent with those that took place earlier? Does every facet of the story come together in the conclusion? Is the viewpoint consistent? The voice? Is the tone right?

Peter was writing a longer fiction about a time in the not-so-distant future when the sale of natural food is banned and people have no choice but to order processed food on-line from the Food Channel. The story is told by the son of a man who works for the illegal network of underground produce markets until he is killed. His truck is blown up by government agents. Following the father's death, the narrator and his family know they have no choice but to accept ordering Food-on-line. Peter ends his story with an advertising jingle that plays continuously on the Food Channel. At the very end are the following lines.

> . . . My pale little sister sings the jingle at the dining table every day while my brother Jason and I boot up the next meal. I have to admit the jingle's pretty catchy though I doubt if Dad would have been caught dead whistling it.

Since the story was sad, to end with a joke, a play on the word *dead* in this case, was out of tone. The narrator seemed too cold and unfeeling. Eventually, Peter changed the last sentence. This one has a wistful quality.

> I have to admit the jingle's pretty catchy though I can only imagine what Dad would say if he were here and caught me whistling it.

Problems with the ending may call attention to problems in other parts as well. It became clear to Peter, for example, that in the climax when his father's truck blows up, the narrator sounds too distant and uncaring.

How will you know when you've found the ending? It will feel right. It will feel like the natural way to close. If you still have trouble, skim the entire piece or reread the beginning before you do more exercises.

A FEW MORE SUGGESTIONS FOR USING THIS PROCESS

Whatever you do, don't let your longer fiction or novel become too serious a pursuit. Remember, nobody is making you do it. This is something you're doing for yourself. Don't try to speed up the process. Don't try to take shortcuts. Impatience will only take you "out" of the writing. While you are writing, the story or novel is the place you choose to live. You can't be *in* the writing at the same time you're wondering how long it will take you to finish. You can't be *in* the writing if you're wishing your novel would end. If you get bored, either put away the work or turn your attention to a different part where you feel energy. Below are more tips for using this process.

Type Your Original Exercises Exactly as They Are Written

At my Sunday afternoon workshop, Donald and Abby said that when they went back and typed out their longhand exercises with all their flaws, *exactly* as they had written them, they found them easier and faster to revise. "Reading the exercises together as I typed really helped," Donald said.

By the time he was ready to revise, he had "the whole thing" in his mind. He knew what to add and what to leave out. He saw where he had repeated himself. Before this, he would revise each exercise as he typed, but that method never gave him a picture of the whole. "It was hard to stop myself from changing things immediately," he said, "but restraining myself paid off in the end."

Notice the Places Where Your Mind Wanders

Patty did just that when she went back over some exercises she had written in her coming-of-age novel about a northern girl who gets involved in the Underground Railroad during the Civil War. Patty found her attention strayed during a section in which her main character, Meg, says good-bye to her best friend, Greta, who is leaving for the front where she is going to be a "regimental daughter" and care for wounded Union troops.

When Patty read the section into a tape recorder, she discovered that the good-bye between Meg and Greta was much too long and sentimental. More important, Patty discovered that she had left out Meg's envy of Greta. Since Meg's desire to play a part in the war is the driving force in the novel, recognizing where her mind wandered led Patty to the heart of the problem. In this scene, Patty needed to give more weight not only to Meg's envy, but also to her frustration about staying at home.

There are many reasons for your mind to wander. The information you're presenting may be unnecessary. It may be repetitive or poorly written. Or maybe your writing lacks contrast. I've found that inexperienced writers in particular tend to create long blocks of narrative. Take note of the exact spot where your attention strays. Then read into a tape recorder. Try breaking up large chunks of description or explanation with actions and events.

Give Problems to Your Unconscious

In the early stages, make your revisions quickly. Don't dwell on any one problem. If you're not sure what to do, leave it alone. Work on another part, and come back later.

My student Will sometimes drives himself crazy thinking about a problem once he's found it. If you are like Will, try this. Allow the problem to stay in your mind without "doing" anything about it. If you must "do" something, give the problem to your unconscious. In your mind, see yourself handing it over. You might try viewing your unconscious as a receptacle of some kind, a bowl or jar perhaps. The act of handing it over to your unconscious may be just what you need to dispel your anxiety and give yourself the space to find a solution.

Allow Yourself to Expand Your Exercises

When you do exercises initially, you may skip over details, dialogue, or actions because you're writing fast and experiencing a rush of words. But once you've written the exercises, you can go back and decide if you want to say more.

If you're attached to your writing, you may find it hard to expand your exercises because you're afraid of destroying certain parts in order to expand. Before you start, make note of the parts you're afraid to lose. Copy them somewhere separate from your exercises. That way they aren't "lost," but they're also not interfering with the work at hand. Later on, the parts you're attached to may be used to trigger more exercises or another story. In the meantime, don't be afraid to cut them out. If you don't, you may stop the flow of your story or novel.

When you expand an exercise, use one or more of the methods described in the last chapter. Either choose a part with energy as a trigger or choose a "Write about . . ." directive. Write as many or as few exercises as you want. To expand part of an exercise, you may set your timer for one, two, or three minutes instead of the usual five. Or you may find that adding a line here and there is enough.

When you finish, be sure to go back and add your new or expanded exercises to your provisional order. Expanding one or more exercises may alter the sequence. Because everything in a work of fiction is connected, the consequence of expanding one part may be difficult to see in advance. One change may be the catalyst for many changes. Expanding a single exercise may alter the entire shape and direction of the whole. This is why it's important to go back. When you do, allow your unconscious to continue playing its part. Allow changes to happen. See your writing as an adventure. Let yourself explore possibilities, though you can be sure in advance that at least some of them will not work.

Save All Your Revisions

If you keep your revisions, you can always change exercises back to the way they were. In order to have this flexibility when you revise, I suggest you save every draft. You may groan upon hearing this, but your discarded drafts are your safety net. You can never fall very far in this process if you can find your way back. Whenever you feel yourself losing energy, retrace your steps and return to the draft that has energy. If you save your revisions, even those of you who still tense up at the thought of revising will have nothing to worry about if you go in the wrong direction every once in a while. Pity the sculptor who carves away a little too much wood or a little too much stone. She can't put the wood or stone back. But you cannot lose your words.

Treat Revision as Play

If your attitude is "It's got to work or I'll die," you'll be giving yourself a great and unnecessary handicap. Not everything you do will turn out the way you want it to immediately. It's okay if it doesn't work today. Eventually it will work. In the meantime, have some fun with it. When you allow yourself to play, you allow things to happen that will surprise you. If you're thinking about how "good" or "bad" the exercises are, you're not connecting with the exercises themselves. If you're nervous or anxious, you're not *feeling* what you wrote. In every mistake, there is something of value. Nothing is wasted. Everything that happens is part of your process. However much time it takes to write your story or novel is the amount of time that is needed.

Vary the Process By Making Notes for Future Revisions

When you review your exercises, instead of revising immediately, you may feel like making notes instead. That's fine unless extensive changes are needed. In that case, making notes will probably be useless. Extensive changes will redirect your writing, so don't wait to revise. If the changes you want to make, however, are not major, and you prefer to make notes, go ahead. But remember that point of view is basic, so you want to feel comfortable with the one you have chosen before you proceed.

As your narrative develops and you learn more about your characters and situations, don't be afraid to go back over your exercises and change the notes you made earlier. In fact, keep changing your notes as the need arises. Allow yourself to cross out and be messy. Your notes need only be readable enough for you to follow when you revise.

Vary the Process By Outlining as You Go

If you outline as you go, don't try to get too far ahead. Sketch out only a scene or two before you write, and allow your outline to be rough. Leave room for the unexpected to happen. Your outline may take the form of a list or a kind of map or chart or even a brief sentence or paragraph. You may even use a conventional format with roman numerals and subheads, as long as you don't make it too elaborate. I suggest you keep the length to less than a page.

If you *must* plan more than a scene or two at a time, keep in mind that your exercises may surprise you. If a new character is introduced or the story takes a turn you didn't expect, this will change how you see the next exercises and the ones that came before. You may find that making outlines is a waste of time. My student Barbara, however, swears by them. They make her feel safe. Paradoxically, the idea of knowing where she's going next gives her the freedom to diverge from her outline whenever she feels like it.

Learn to Skim

Going back over your exercises is not as much trouble as it may seem. Donald, for example, would write a few exercises, which he would revise or make notes on, depending upon his mood; then he would go back over previous groups of exercises and revise them in light of the new ones.

As Donald's novel developed, the number of exercises grew. At one point, he had about sixty. It was difficult to know the exact number because by that time, many of the exercises had been "blended," or extensively changed.

Did he carefully reread all his exercises each time before writing the next six? No. Once you've read a group of exercises two or three times, they will be in your head unless you've taken a long break from your work. Instead of rereading every one, learn to skim. Do it fast. Try to get a sense of the *shape* of your piece so far. Hold it in your mind. When you do so, parts that feel wrong may stand out. Pay attention to your feelings as you skim. Stop only when you find something bothersome. When you do stop, don't spend a lot of time revising or changing your notes. Pause and think for a few minutes, but not longer. If the solution doesn't come quickly, mark the spot and go on. When your early draft is finished you'll come back and figure it out. You don't want to interfere with the forward movement of your story or novel. What you want to do is integrate each part as you go.

TEN

REFINING LONGER FICTION

Y ou are ready to start the process of refining when you have written a draft of your story or novel that goes from beginning to end. I hesitate to call this draft a *first* draft. If you have followed the method introduced in the last chapter and gone back over each group of exercises, you have been revising your manuscript all along. So when I talk about a first draft, I'm not talking about a draft of raw or totally unrevised exercises, I'm talking about a draft of the *entire* story or novel that is well on its way.

This draft is still rough, but the basic story line and structure are in place. If someone asked, you could say in a sentence or two what your story or novel is about. You know who is telling it, the basic conflict, the big events. When you try to visualize the whole, you have a sense of the overall shape. You see the story build, you know more or less what happens at the climax, and you may even see the story taper off and come to an end, though at this point, the ending may be nothing more than a crudely rendered idea.

As you read this, you may find yourself having qualms about the structure or story line, the conflict, climax, or point of view. If this is the case, return to chapter nine. Don't try to rush the process. Give yourself the time you need. If, however, you have established the basics of your story, read on.

A Note About Creating Chapters
Before I discuss refining your work, I would like to touch on creating chapters. So far, I have not used the word *chapter* in this book because

I felt it would be confusing to use this word along with *exercises* and *scenes*. This is a good time, however, to consider making chapters if you haven't already done so.

Some of you may find that breaks occur naturally as you write. Donald, for instance, found himself making a chapter out of every scene. Each scene included anywhere from eight to thirteen exercises. You, too, may choose to break a chapter after every scene. You may even make one out of every exercise. You may vary the lengths of your chapters. You may choose to title them or not.

Experiment with chapter breaks, looking for places to stop. See where they work best. This is not a mechanical process. When you consider your novel in terms of chapters, see each one as a unit that completes something but, at the same time, opens the door to whatever lies ahead.

THE PROCESS OF REFINING

The process of refining is as important as the initial process of getting your words down. Being able to handle and control language, however, is not necessarily synonymous with being able to tell a good story. Chris, for example, had no problem getting his coming-of-age novel on paper. As I mentioned earlier, his particular writing process needed fifteen-minute exercises rather than the usual five. The material came to him in great bursts. Energy was certainly not his problem. He also knew by instinct how to tell a story and create characters who were surprising, sympathetic, and believable enough to keep the reader's interest. In fact, the novel had so much drive and energy and the story line and characters were so strong that when Chris, a former actor, read aloud from his work—his delivery was an asset, too—the clumsiness of the prose was easy to overlook.

I couldn't overlook it, however, when I read the novel carefully by myself. Errors in grammar, punctuation, and spelling were easy to spot. But these were not all of Chris' problems. Besides dangling modifiers, run-on sentences, misplaced commas, and clichés, I found misused words, awkward phrases, a couple of rambling chapters, an overwritten scene, and too much explanation in the whole. Chris had a lot of refining to do.

What exactly is refining? Refining is the process of perfecting your story or novel. It's a process of cutting words, adding words, substituting words, and moving them around, singly or in chunks. It's a process of introducing subtleties and making distinctions as well as cutting every word that is superfluous. Refining is the process that comes after the fear of getting down the basics subsides.

The Close-Up View

The act of refining is for some writers the most enjoyable part of the fiction-writing process. Until now you have had to restrain yourself from finishing each part or exercise because your narrative was still in a process of change. At this point, however, you are ready to tackle the problems *within* each part. You have the chance to write those beautiful sentences, to concern yourself with nuances and subtleties that would have gotten in your way before.

But be careful not to go overboard. By this I mean that some strictures still apply. You don't, for example, want any words in your story or novel to be there without reason. You don't want to overwrite or change the voice you have established. Relating each sentence, each paragraph, to the larger unit of the exercise, the scene, or the chapter, and finally to the whole, will help you see your writing in perspective. A sentence alone may be beautifully crafted, but unless it relates to the whole, it is expendable.

When you refine your fiction, you examine each part carefully. You examine each paragraph and look at the place each paragraph breaks: Where a paragraph breaks contributes to the rhythm. You look at each sentence in terms of structure, length, and rhythm. You look at your word choices, and you ask yourself if each sentence has the meaning you intended.

Your experience revising the short short will pay off when you refine a longer fiction. The common problems you encountered with the shorter form will be encountered here as well. As you refine your longer work, be sure to refer to chapter five, "Shaping and Polishing Short Short Stories," in the first section of this book.

Before you are ready to concentrate on each part of your draft, however, you need to see it as a whole.

Seeing the Whole

Skim through the entire manuscript quickly. As you do so, mark sections, paragraphs, sentences, or phrases that bother you, but don't stop in the middle of reading to take notes or make changes because this will break up the story in your mind, and what you want to do is grasp it in its entirety.

Problems are likely to stand out when you see the draft as a whole, so when you finish, ask yourself, Do the parts fit together smoothly? Do connections still need to be made? Pay attention to the parts that stay in your mind.

If you have trouble identifying problems while you skim, go back and read the manuscript more carefully. Besides grammatical errors, you are likely to find other problems you missed before. Some of these will feel familiar. You may have encountered the same or similar ones in earlier stages of your manuscript. Among the most common at this stage are

- beginnings that still go on and on
- characters that have been introduced, then dropped
- scenes that need to be built
- rambling chapters
- overwritten scenes
- dialogue that is out of character
- scenes that drag
- parts that need transitions or transitions that are long or abrupt
- actions that need to be set up earlier
- subplots that are started but never developed
- characters that need to be fleshed out
- narrative scenes that would work better as action

You may need to refer to chapter nine in order to solve some of them.

Even in the final stages, it's best to expect the unexpected. This is not a negative way of looking at your work, but rather one that keeps you open, that allows you to see opportunities and possibilities you may not have been aware of in earlier stages. The more you write, the more you see. Refining is not a neat and tidy process. It means going back and forth over your manuscript again and again. One change may lead to others you didn't foresee.

Use common sense. Don't worry about commas before you cut that long-winded beginning, build that scene, or figure out what else is wrong.

Balancing the Parts

In a short short, problems exist within a small context, but in a longer work, some problems can't be seen by focusing on a single part. You can't tell if there is too much explanation or too little action, for example, unless you have a picture in your mind of the entire manuscript. You need to see each part in relation to the whole. This is a subtle process that involves feeling rather than thinking.

A piece of fiction with ideal proportions is one in which the ratio of description, action, explanation and dialogue feels harmonious. There is no recipe I can give you for this. Every story is different. For example, you may write a novel that is mainly dialogue. It may have little description, action, or explanation and still feel harmonious.

If you are unsure of the difference between explanation and description, think of this phrase when you think of an explanation: "This is so because. . . ."

When you have the right amount of these four elements, the story doesn't slow down or stop unexpectedly. If you are bored, for example, see this as a sign that the parts are out of balance. You may need contrast. You may have too much explanation or description, and not enough action or dialogue.

Focus on each element. Ask yourself the following questions:

- Is there too much or too little description?
- Is there too much or too little action?
- Is there too much or too little explanation?
- Is there too much or too little dialogue?

Keep in mind that first novels often suffer from too much explanation, which is another way of saying there is too much telling and not enough showing.

If you have too much explanation or description and you need to turn a narrative passage into an action scene, use a five-minute exercise. Take a word, a phrase, or a sentence from the section you wish to change and use it to trigger an exercise. Direct yourself to writing an action scene. Show instead of tell. Be sure to read over the passage before you start. The unexpected may happen, but you're not *trying* to write something different; you're simply giving dimension to what you already have.

Bring your new exercises up to the same level as the rest of your draft, but don't try to polish them before you polish the rest of your manuscript.

Refining Part by Part

After you have skimmed the entire manuscript and identified as many problems as you can, you are ready to refine your manuscript, part by part. I define a part here as an exercise, scene, or chapter.

As you refine, you need to see each word, each sentence, each paragraph alone *and* in context. You need to see how each part fits in the whole. Remember, a change that works in a particular scene may not work in terms of the entire manuscript.

Start at the beginning. Read over the entire portion you intend to refine. You may begin by going through it and making the changes that come most easily, then work your way gradually to more difficult problems that will take more time and effort. Or you may correct each problem as it arises regardless of whether it is difficult or easy. When you've gone as far as you can, you may do a line-by-line reading from the top to check for final errors.

Refining means more than changing a word, phrase, sentence, or paragraph. It often means altering what comes before and after the parts you have changed as well. Nothing exists independently. In fact, a story or novel may be compared to the body. When you move one part, you affect others too. When you turn your head, for example, your neck moves, your shoulders move, your torso shifts its position, and so on. As I said earlier, writing is organic. A few sentences added in one part of a story, for instance, may affect the story more than you imagined.

When you refine part by part, it's easy to lose sight of the whole, to get lost in details, especially when you're trying to perfect each one. This is why it's important to look at your work from a distance at regular intervals.

Choose random sections to read aloud as you work, even if it is just a paragraph or two here and there. Read a passage from the beginning, for example, as you work on a section toward the middle. Then read a passage near the end. This will help you keep control of the whole as you work part by part. Hearing these disparate excerpts will give you the certainty that you haven't lapsed into a different voice, point of view, or style. Consider these as "checkups" on your work.

It's likely you will refine each part of your manuscript a number of times. Each time you do so, you may see it a little differently. As I said, this is not a tidy process. You may find yourself cutting chunks of a chapter *after* you've polished it. Does this mean that polishing the chapter was a waste of time? I would say no. Everything that happens in your story or novel is part of your process. Consider every bit of writing that you do as practice. It's through practice that writers hone their skills. See the wrong steps you take as those that enable you to find the right ones.

What to Do When You Don't Know What's Wrong

How will you recognize the minor problems in your fiction? You will *feel* that something is wrong. As I've said over and over in this book, listen to your feelings, even though you may not know exactly what is wrong or why something doesn't work. Try to identify as closely as possible the page, paragraph, sentence, or word that is bothering you. The more precise you can be the better. If you can identify only the general area where you have a problem, a chapter, for instance, let that chapter brew in your unconscious. You may do this in several different ways. Read it over silently a couple of times. Read it into a tape recorder, or, better yet, read it to someone else out loud. Even if the listener doesn't know a whole lot about writing, his presence or attention may be enough to spark a clue. If you're still not sure what's wrong, put the manuscript away for a while or work on a different part.

You may also hand the problem area to your unconscious before you go to sleep at night. Don't be afraid to ask your unconscious to tell you exactly what is wrong and what to do about it. My student Barbara swears that she wakes up with the answers, though she says it doesn't always work the first time. Whether or not you deliberately give the problem area to your unconscious, that part of your mind will work on it anyway. You may be in the middle of doing an errand or having coffee or glancing through a magazine when you suddenly understand what's wrong with the chapter you're troubled by. It's important not to dwell on the problem. It's easy to drive yourself crazy.

When my student Will starts to get obsessed, I tell him to go to the gym. A good workout takes his mind off his writing. Any activity— whether it is cooking, making love, or watching a video—is good if it takes your mind off your problem.

It may be that once you identify the trouble, you discover that it is larger than you thought. In fact, it may mean going back to the basic structure or story line or conflict. If this is the case, don't try to fudge the problem. Go back to the previous chapter. This is not a step backward. You needed to get to this point in order to see the difficulty, which you were able to identify through the experience of working on your story.

How to Know What Works

When you *lose* yourself in a story or novel, you are so immersed in what you are reading you are no longer aware of words on the page. Instead, you see with the narrator's eyes. You see, hear, feel, touch, and smell whatever the characters see, hear, feel, touch, and smell. When you enter the world the writer has created, you're aware of nothing else. You forget your room, noises from the street, bills you have to pay, errands you have to run, deadlines you have to meet.

Notice in your own fiction those parts where you are able to lose yourself. Those are the parts that work. Use them as models. Ask yourself, How are these sections different from the rest of my manuscript?

Throughout this book, I've been telling you to listen to your feelings. What works in your writing is what *feels* right. Here, however, I am going one step further by saying that when a story or novel works, *it exists independent of the writer.* When you lose yourself in your writing, you are owning up to the fact that your fiction has a life of its own.

How to Know When to Stop

There comes a point when you've improved your piece as much as you can. You can't go any further. Any changes you make now will work against you. If you're listening to your feelings, you will recognize this point and stop. If you're nervous and fearful, you're likely to keep going. If you go beyond this point, you will find that you are making it worse. You are still making changes, but the changes no longer improve the piece. They don't feel right. They don't work.

When the process begins to go backward, think of this as the story's or novel's way of telling you this is as good as it gets. Finishing often means taking your hands off the work and accepting it, knowing that you have taken it as far as you can. Some of you may need to step over this limit to know that you have passed the point of improvement. If you have passed this point, go back through your revisions and find the last ones that worked well. This won't be a big problem if you've been saving your revisions all along as I suggested in the previous chapter. If your earlier drafts are dated or numbered, you'll be able to see exactly when and where you went off the track. Once you have reinstated the passages you erroneously discarded, allow yourself to let go of your work even if it feels less than perfect. The standards you are setting for yourself may be too high. If you put your manuscript aside for several weeks, then read it again, you may find yourself pleasantly surprised.

AN EXAMPLE OF THE REFINING PROCESS

My student Donald began his novel without a plan. In a five-minute "Write about . . ." exercise, he invented two characters who sparked his interest. As I mentioned earlier, Brian is a young gay man. Joan is an older Englishwoman living in a large apartment on Manhattan's upper west side. She rents a room to Brian.

When Donald began doing exercises, he knew very little about the characters. In spite of his uncertainty, he allowed himself to be led by his unconscious and wrote one five-minute exercise after another.

The unconscious is not always right, however. While developing the characters and exploring their relationship, Donald wrote many exercises that he discarded, some immediately, others later on, as the direction of his novel slowly emerged. Each "misfired" exercise, however, helped Donald find his way.

At first, the beginning was too long and the characters were flat. Donald rarely touched upon their motives, their thoughts, their wishes, their fears, their dreams. He was rarely *inside* their heads.

He was aware that many questions needed to be answered. Nevertheless, he kept going *because there was energy*. He didn't tell himself, "Well, this isn't right, and this isn't right, and this isn't right, so why bother?" Instead, he took chances. He wasn't "wed" to his words, so he was flexible enough to change or abandon parts when the need arose.

At first, the novel began with Brian answering an ad that Joan had placed in the newspaper under Rooms for Rent. The *real* beginning, however, was written later in a set of five-minute exercises that take place when Brian first comes to New York from Ohio and stays with his high school friend Martha, who helps him land a job in the display department of Macy's where she works.

Notes on the Exercises

The eight five-minute exercises below became chapter seven. They were written in response to the directive "What happens next?" Donald didn't have to worry about putting them in sequence because all but one, mini-exercise three, were written in chronological order. At the time they were written, about fifty pages preceded them. Many of those pages were subsequently cut.

When Brian comes to New York in chapter one and crashes with his old friend Martha, the narrator says that Brian is lazy. He likes to have people take care of him. He wishes that Martha would find him an apartment.

The exercises for chapter seven take place soon after Brian has moved into Joan's apartment. Brian and Joan are just getting to know each other. But even at this early stage, we see signs of the conflict to come. Brian longs to be taken care of, but he knows that if he gives in to this impulse, he risks losing the freedom he's come to New York to find.

Brian learns that Joan has a son. Later in the novel, Bobby, as he is called, is the catalyst for bringing Joan and Brian back together after he's moved out.

The exercises below appear as they did in Donald's first complete draft, which was still rough, though not completely unrevised. If you compare the exercises with the refined chapter, you will see the changes and additions. On the pages following the refined chapter, you will find notes that tell you what was done and why.

The Exercises

Exercise 1

It was Brian's second week in Joan's apartment. His room was just the way he wanted and he was settling into his routine.

Every night he'd come home from work, go into his room, turn on the tv, and flop on his bed for a nice nap during the news. A few nights, he had been stirred from his nap by the timid tapping of Joan's fingers on his door, followed by her less timid "Brian, Brian, are you there?"

One night, she wanted to show him the latest project from her icon painting class. Another night, she wanted him to carry some heavy boxes out of her bedroom into the spare bedroom. He didn't really mind, because Joan never ran out of little stories and anecdotes.

Exercise 2

Brian had just started to doze off during the 6:30 news when he heard a timid tapping at his door, followed by a less timid, "Brian, Brian, are you there?" It was time for Joan's nightly visit. He was trying to rouse himself to full consciousness, and confusedly wondered what she wanted this time. Did she want to show him another one of her projects from her icon painting class? Or maybe she wanted him to move another one of the seemingly endless number of boxes she had stored away all over the apt. He had been living at Joan's apartment for two weeks now and he had gotten used to this routine.

Exercise 3
(written later and inserted)

Joan liked to use the pretense of show and tell or assistance on some small chore as an entree into a chance to talk to Brian. He suspected that under her curmudgeonly front she was lonely. He had noticed that she never got phone calls, and since he had moved in, she had spent every evening home alone as far as he could tell.

Exercise 4

This evening, he was particularly tired since he had been out late with Martha the night before, and it had been a hard day at work. All he wanted was to be alone and relax—maybe if he didn't answer her she'd go away. If she asked about it later, he could say he had been asleep.

"Brian," came Joan's voice through the door. "Are you there?"

It was no use. He was awake now. "Yes?" he called out, still lying on his back on his bed.

"Oh, you're there. I was just wondering if you'd like to share my dinner with me? I'm frying some chicken and there's more than I can eat by myself."

Brian perked up when he heard this. Now he felt a little guilty. "That sounds nice," he said, as he got off the bed. He opened the door to look at Joan, standing in the service area outside his room. "I was wondering what I was going to eat for dinner," he said.

Exercise 5

He followed Joan around the corner into the kitchen.

"I just have to fry these legs," she said, as she walked over to the stove. "I thought I'd treat myself tonight. I also bought some lettuce for a salad."

Brian looked at the head of lettuce laying on the counter. "Do you want me to do the salad?" he asked. "I have some tomatoes I can add to it."

He and Joan had separate refrigerators. They were positioned across from one another in the hall outside Brian's room. Joan's was new and white, and Brian's was older and avocado colored. By now he had learned that Joan liked to have two or more of the same thing. Brian had learned by now that Joan thought that it was always good to have two of something, and even better to have three.

Exercise 6

"That would be lovely," Joan said, sounding truly grateful.

Brian could tell that making this meal was quite an effort for her. He came back to the sink just in time to see Joan draining the contents of a can of mandarin oranges onto the chicken legs that were arranged in a skillet on the stove. Joan had a habit of looking surprised whenever she had something in her hand—and that's how she looked as she dumped the oranges. Her arm was held out straight, and she looked surprised when the oranges fell out with a splash. She seemed genuinely surprised that they had landed in the skillet at all. She looked at him and saw him watching her. "Chicken a l'orange," she said, rolling her eyes and wiggling her head in a la-de-da fashion. "I know it's not in anymore to use tinned fruit, but I adore mandarin oranges and you can't get them this time of year."

Exercise 7

"My grandmother always buys canned peaches," Brian said, by way of extenuating Joan's taste. He didn't add that he couldn't stand the texture of canned fruit.

"I studied cooking with one of the best chefs in NY back in the fifties. It's where Craig Claiborne and everyone else went," she said, as she moved the sizzling chicken legs around in the disintegrating orange slices in their light syrup.

"Oh, that's impressive," Brian said, as he was slicing the tomatoes at the counter. "Were you ever a chef?"

"No, not really. My husband only liked certain things. You know, meat and potatoes," she said with a shrug. "It was all wasted on him. And then Bobby was born so of course, I couldn't work."

Exercise 8

"Bobby. Do you have a son?" Brian said, surprised. Joan had never mentioned this before. He wondered for a split second if he had died or something—he wasn't ready for hearing something depressing like that.

"Of course. You didn't know. That's his room across from mine," Joan said, referring to what Brian recognized as the door that was always shut. He thought it was a closet. "Where is he?" Brian asked.

"Away at school. He's at John Reed College in Oregon. His father's paying for it, of course, since it's the least he can do under the circumstances."

Brian wasn't sure what their circumstances were, he was just so taken aback by the idea of someone not talking about their son away at school. Joan was the least maternal seeming person he could imagine. "How old is he?" he asked.

"Twenty-one. He'll be graduating next June and then he'll be back here which I'm in no hurry for I can assure you. He'll be back here expecting me to cook meals for him and he'll always have his hand out for money. I've been strongly encouraging him to stay on for his master's degree but he's made up his mind he's coming back," she said, sighing.

The Refined Chapter

Chapter 7

It was Brian's second week in Joan's apartment. His room was just the way he wanted and he was settling into his routine. Every night he'd come home from work, go into his room, turn on the tv, and flop on his bed for a pleasant nap during the news. This evening he was particularly tired since he had been out late with Martha the night before, and it had been a hard day at work. All he wanted to do was be alone and relax.

He had just started to doze off during the 6:30 news when he heard a timid tapping at the door, followed by a less timid, "Brian? Brian? Are you there?"

What did Joan want this time? he wondered, trying to rouse himself. One night she wanted to show him the latest project from her icon painting class. Another night she asked him to move some of the heavy cartons she kept stored all over the apartment.

He suspected that under her crankiness she was lonely. He noticed that she rarely got phone calls, and as far as he could tell, she had spent every evening alone since he had arrived.

Maybe if he didn't answer, she'd go away, he thought. Later, he could say that he'd been sleeping.

"Brian?" came Joan's voice a little more insistently. "Are you there?"

It was no use. He had to see what she wanted now that he was fully awake.

"Yes?" he called out from his bed.

"Oh, you *are* there," she said. "I was just wondering if you'd like to share my dinner with me. I'm going to fry some chicken legs. I have more than I can eat."

Brian perked up when he heard this. He also felt a little guilty. He rose quickly and opened the door. Joan was standing in the hallway. "You haven't had dinner yet, have you?" she asked.

"No, I haven't. Thank you," he said. So far they had taken their meals separately. He usually liked to wait until he was sure he had the kitchen to himself, but he was so tired tonight that he was truly grateful to have her cook for him.

He followed Joan through the hallway to the kitchen.

"It won't take long to fry these legs," Joan said, walking over to the stove. "I bought some lettuce to make a salad too." She put the chicken in a well-used skillet.

Brian looked at the head of lettuce lying on the counter. "Do you want me to do the salad?" he asked. "I have some tomatoes in my refrigerator."

"That sounds lovely," Joan said, as though it had never occurred to her to put tomatoes in a salad.

Brian could tell that making this meal was quite an effort for her.

He and Joan had separate refrigerators. They were positioned across from one another in the hall outside Brian's room. Joan's was new and white, his was older and harvest gold. He had learned by now that Joan thought it was good to have two of things, and even better to have three.

He returned with the tomatoes in time to see Joan dumping a can of mandarin orange slices over the chicken legs. To avoid getting splashed, she held the can as far from her body as possible. But when the fruit hit the pan, she seemed genuinely surprised to see it land in the skillet at all. She looked up to see him watching her.

"Chicken a l'orange," she said. "I know it's not *in* these days to eat things out of tins, but I *adore* mandarin oranges. You can't get them fresh this time of year. I remember during the war when we were happy to eat anything out of a tin."

"My grandmother always eats canned peaches," Brian said. What he didn't say was that he couldn't stand the texture of canned fruit. He went on washing the lettuce leaves in the sink, and watched her out of the corner of his eye. She was poking the chicken around in the skillet, as it sizzled in the light syrup and dissolving orange slices. He supposed it was a good sign that it smelled good because it certainly didn't look appetizing.

"Back in the fifties, I studied cooking at one of the best schools in New York City," Joan said. "The same school where Craig Claiborne studied."

Brian looked dubiously at the skillet and said, "Really? That's impressive." He began slicing the tomatoes on the counter. "Were you ever a chef?"

"No, not really. My husband Peter only liked meat and potatoes," she said, with a shrug. "It was all wasted on him. And then Bobby was born so I couldn't work."

"Bobby? You have a son?" Brian asked, surprised. But as soon as he asked, he was afraid to hear the answer. What if Bobby was dead? Or put away in a home.

"Haven't I mentioned him before? His room is the one across from mine," Joan said, referring to what Brian had assumed was just another closet.

"Where is he now?"

"He's away at school," Joan replied. "John Reed College in Oregon. His father's paying for it. It's the least he can do under the circumstances."

Brian assumed the *circumstances* were Joan's and Peter's divorce, but he was so surprised to hear that Joan had a son— he couldn't imagine anyone less maternal—that he knew he shouldn't assume anything.

"How old is he?" Brian asked, slicing another tomato. He wondered if Bobby was cute, but that wasn't the kind of question you ask someone's mother.

"Twenty-one. He'll be graduating next June. Then he'll be back here, with his hand out for money, expecting me to cook his meals. I keep telling him to stay out there and get his Master's Degree but he won't listen. I *dread* having him home!"

Brian was more than a bit shocked to hear Joan speak so disparagingly about her son. He was thinking that even his own mother, cold as she was, would never speak of him like that, especially to a near-stranger, even if she did share Joan's sentiments, which might well be the case.

Notes on Refining the Exercises

Exactly how this chapter fits into the whole is impossible to show without reprinting the complete work. Nevertheless, I thought it might be helpful to see part of the process. For the sake of brevity, I mention here only those changes and additions that need some clarification. I haven't mentioned minor cuts or minor changes in grammar, spelling, or punctuation.

After reading the exercises aloud in class and making brief notes based on suggestions made by my students and myself, Donald corrected problems in the order in which he found them. Some of his best writing "happened" while he was refining. This is proof that the unconscious doesn't stop working when you use your rational mind.

He began the process by looking closely at the first two exercises. He had written the word *repetition* in the margins. Both exercises cover the same material, but each has a different tone. In the light of what we've learned about Brian in the preceding chapters, the tone of exercise one rings false. Brian claims he doesn't mind Joan's visits, but we already know he has a sharp eye, a dry wit, and little tolerance for other people's foibles. At best, he has mixed feelings about Joan. In the second exercise, we feel Brian's annoyance when she wakes him up. This response feels true. In the same exercise, Joan's nightly intrusions seem extreme so early in the novel. A novel needs to build gradually. Brian stands to lose his credibility if Joan is very intrusive from the start. We will wonder why Brian doesn't find another room and move out.

Donald's refined chapter starts off unchanged. He clues us into Brian's routine, but then adds the beginning of exercise four, where he says that Brian is tired, in order to set the stage for Joan tapping on his door. He is giving more background when he says that Joan has intruded twice since he's moved in.

Near the opening line of mini-exercise three, the word *repetition* again appeared in Donald's notes. He's already hinted that Joan looks for excuses to talk to Brian, so he doesn't need to say it again. More important is Brian's insight that Joan is lonely. The awkward phrase "curmudgeonly front" he changed to "crankiness."

Starting with exercise four, Donald mainly uses dialogue to advance the story. In the refined version, Donald expands this exercise and shows just how reticent Brian is by revealing that he usually waited until the kitchen was empty to have dinner.

In the margins of exercise six, Donald had written the words *awkward description*. The writing was too clumsy and imprecise for us to clearly visualize Joan "dumping" the mandarin orange slices into the skillet. The description is important because it catches Joan off guard and allows us to see a little more of her eccentricity. The oddness of her gestures gives weight to Brian's claim that this meal is an effort for her to make. To avoid making Joan look ridiculous, however, Donald cut the description of her "rolling her eyes" and so on.

In his rewrites of exercises seven and eight, Donald makes the reader privy to more of the thoughts and feelings Brian keeps hidden from Joan. Tension is created by the fact that his outward behavior is often at odds with his inner life. In the rewrite of exercise seven, Brian watches Joan "out of the corner of his eye" while washing the lettuce. This simple gesture lets the reader glimpse the secretive and mistrustful side of Brian's nature. Donald adds a touch of humor to the refined version of exercise eight, however, when Brian wonders if Bobby is cute. The shock Brian feels when Joan talks about her feelings for her son sparked Donald to write the last lines, revealing the coldness of Brian's mother, which gives us some insight into Brian's past.

Besides the contrast between Brian's inner life and outward behavior, there is the contrast between Joan and Brian. She lets her feelings hang out. These contrasts give life to the characters and save this chapter from the flatness that may result when writers restrict themselves to events that take place solely on the surface. This is why every line showing us what the characters think and feel is important. Keeping this in mind, Donald continues to refine his manuscript as of this writing.

FINAL THOUGHTS

As I mentioned a little earlier, your unconscious doesn't stop working just because you are using your rational mind. Refining is a process that embraces both your conscious *and* unconscious. Some of your best lines may "happen" when, in the midst of trying to figure something out, you let your mind wander.

The more you use this method, the easier you will shift from one mode to another. As I've said, the unconscious is always working. It's going on even while you're using your critical faculties. Whether you *attend* to it or not is your choice. Even in the midst of the most trying problems, you have the possibility of drifting off and giving your conscious mind a rest. This change of focus may be just what you need to find a solution.

As I was nearing the end of this book, I asked several of my students what they liked best about the five-minute method. Liz said she liked that she could combine taking risks and trusting her unconscious with working step-by-step in a rational, methodical way. All the books she had read on writing fiction emphasized one approach or the other, she said. Susan, Donald, and Wanda agreed. Some books advised them to let it all hang out while other books advised them to plan every move.

One part of your mind is always taking precedence over the other unless you are stuck. Writer's block is what happens when the conscious mind competes with the unconscious and both try to occupy the same space at the same time.

When you use the five-minute method, you recognize that the unconscious and the conscious mind each has a place in the process of writing fiction. You recognize the difference between the two, and you allow yourself to use both of them.

ABOUT THE AUTHOR

Roberta Allen is the author of two collections of short fiction, *The Traveling Woman* (Vehicle Editions, 1986) and *Certain People* (Coffee House Press, 1997); a novella in short short stories, *The Daughter* (Autonomedia, 1992); and a memoir, *Amazon Dream* (City Lights, 1993). Allen is on the faculty of The New School for Social Research and also teaches at New York University, at The Writer's Voice, and in private workshops. She is also an established visual artist. Her work has been exhibited worldwide, and is included in the collection of the Metropolitan Museum of Art.

INDEX